Reagan the Man,
the President

Reagan the Man, the President

Hedrick Smith

Adam Clymer

Leonard Silk

Robert Lindsey

Richard Burt

Macmillan Publishing Co., Inc.
NEW YORK

ACKNOWLEDGEMENTS

The authors would like to thank the following for their assistance: Richard V. Allen, James A. Baker, III, J. Michael Boskin, William Boyarsky, Lou Cannon, Justin W. Dart, Michael Deaver, Alan Greenspan, Congressman Jack Kemp, James Lake, Drew Lewis, Edwin Meese, III, Robert Mundell, Lyn Nofziger, John P. Sears, George P. Shultz, William French Smith, William Timmons, Holmes P. Tuttle, William R. Van Cleave, Charls E. Walker, Jude Wanniski, Caspar Weinberger, and Richard Wirthlin.

Also: Linda Amster, Donna Anderson, John Finney, Judy Greenfeld, Ferne Horner, Linda Lake, Pam Lyons, Eden-Lee Murray, Sunday Orme, and Wallace Turner.

Roger Jellinek of New York Times Books deserves a special word of thanks for his thoughtful and creative editing of several manuscripts under great time pressures. And a special tip of the hat to Sam Summerlin, who conceived the idea and kept it alive, and to Paul Gendelman, who carried the word to the world.

Copyright © 1980 by NYT Productions

Macmillan Publishing Co., Inc.
866 Third Avenue, New York, N.Y. 10022
Collier Macmillan Canada, Ltd.

Library of Congress Catalog Card Number: 8027540

10 9 8 7 6 5 4 3 2 1

Printed in the United States of America

Editors for the *The New York Times* Company:
Howard Angione, Roger Jellinek, Sam Summerlin.

Contents

Introduction:
A Historic Opportunity

Hedrick Smith

We have arrived at a fascinating and quite remarkable moment in American political history. A sixty-nine-year-old man who has spent most of his working life in another profession has captured the Presidency and won the opportunity to lead a political revolution. Or more precisely, a conservative political Reformation that seeks to redirect the role of government in American life and perhaps to reshape the national political landscape for the rest of the century.

For Ronald Wilson Reagan is a crusader, the first missionary conservative to win the White House since Franklin D. Roosevelt defeated Herbert Hoover in 1932 and launched a literal revolution of governmental activism and Democratic Party dominance that has lasted nearly fifty years. Now comes another reformer preaching the gospel that government is not the solution but part of the problem, promising an era of national renewal based on less government, and projecting that same jaunty, smiling self-confidence as Roosevelt in the teeth of national cynicism and despair.

The challenge is monumental. Ronald Reagan takes office at

1

a time when the wellsprings of public confidence have nearly run dry and the yearning for America to regain control of its destiny is palpable across the land. A decade ago, the seemingly endless agony of Vietnam sapped the nation's strength and morale and left the crippling sensation that something had gone profoundly wrong. The seizure of American hostages in Iran sharpened the pain of national humiliation. The fifty-two hostages, pawns in the byzantine internal feuding in Iran, became the concrete metaphor for America's abiding sense of impotence. It was shattering to the national ego when the rescue attempt last August aborted because vaunted American technology broke down in the Iranian desert.

At home, the nation's economic afflictions have seemed beyond the wit of thinkers to diagnose properly or the power of policy-makers to cure. Three Presidents have ventured forth to do battle with the twin-headed monster of inflation and unemployment and have ultimately been devoured by that dragon. America's aging industry loses out all too often to foreign competitors. Growing dependence on imported oil has been an insistent reminder of the limits of the country's once apparently inexhaustible resources and its vulnerability to the leverage of alien powers. Americans may joke about the Ayatollah, about buying Sony TV sets and Toyota cars while unemployment rises in Detroit, or about foreigners purchasing American banks and rich Midwestern farmland, but it is brittle laughter.

In the wake of Vietnam and Watergate, the powers of the Presidency are at ebb tide. Watergate undermined public confidence in politics and politicians. Congressional assertiveness matched foreign assertiveness. For eight of the past twelve years, the government stood stalemated by Democratic control of Congress and Republican control of the White House. Yet even with both branches in Democratic hands under Jimmy Carter, power was so fragmented that special interests had a field day with their single-minded obstructionism because the system lacked the guiding direction of a cohesive, purposeful, and disciplined ruling party. Jimmy Carter had ambitions for an energetic Presidency but proved too inexperienced, too apolitical, too uncertain a leader to generate a governing coalition. The seventies demanded greatness but spawned mediocrity reminiscent of the nineteenth-century stewardships of Zachary Taylor, Millard Fillmore, Franklin Pierce, and James Buchanan.

Now, with the characteristic optimism of the newly elected, the Reagan entourage proclaims its power to overcome the national disarray and to set a new and positive course. Bolstered by the unexpected Republican majority in the Senate and thirty-three new seats in the House of Representatives alongside Reagan's own stunning electoral landslide, Republicans claim a mandate for a bold experiment in conservatism — deep tax cuts, defense increases, a real rollback of Federal regulations, reduced environmental restraints on energy production, reduction of the size and scope of government, and proud restoration of the vigor and vitality of free enterprise.

Party leaders like Bill Brock, the national chairman, think at long last that they discern the end of the Democratic era and perceive the potential for a fundamental political realignment that will make the Republicans the dominant party in America for many years to come. To the traditional Republican base in the West and among white Protestant farmers, small businessmen, and affluent suburbanites, they took in new legions of disaffected Southerners, Catholics, Jews, and ethnic urban blue-collar workers. On Capitol Hill, right-wingers talk confidently of a conservative tide that has swept away such prominent liberal Democrats as Senators George McGovern of South Dakota, Frank Church of Idaho, John Culver of Iowa, and Birch Bayh of Indiana, champions of governmental activism and liberal internationalism in the Congress. The stock market has bubbled euphorically.

Yet doubts linger. Once before, when Dwight Eisenhower won the Presidency in 1952 after twenty years of Democratic rule, the Republicans thought they had overturned Roosevelt's powerful New Deal coalition, heralding a new political period. Later, in 1968, Richard Nixon thought that his ascendancy had signaled a turning point for the Republican Party. But in neither case was a political watershed crossed. Democrats and their policies were later restored, and the nation muddled on without turning a historic corner.

Now, for all the force of the new Republican conquests, the election of 1980 seems less an irreversible ideological tidal wave than a massive vote of protest against the status quo, an explosion of voter frustration against the incumbents that could turn against the Republicans four years hence if they do not satisfy the electorate. "We have brought together the elements of a new coalition," observed Bill Brock, the Republican chairman. "The cementing of that coalition depends on our performance in office. We've got to act with some urgency to deal with the problems on which people voted — unemployment and inflation."

The dimensions of the Reagan victory in November will undoubtedly make the new Congress more pliable, but they will not stifle the opposition. One liberal Democrat who survived the Republican sweep, Senator Gary Hart of Colorado, put a stark challenge to the new leadership on economic policy. "I give the Reagan administration about eighteen to twenty-four months to prove it doesn't have any answers either," Hart declared.

The paradox is that with Republican control of the Senate, Reagan may have won too much. Democrats cannot be blamed for his failures and Republicans may be too slow to shed the dissident habits of opposition. They may be too unaccustomed to the responsibilities of governing to pull together for Reagan's grand design. The new President may find his major objectives caught in a crossfire between moderates and liberals who resist his emphasis on defense and budget-cutting and right-wingers who want to veer off on tangents like abortion and school prayers.

Reagan, having preached the politics of hope, has raised high expectations. He has set standards that he will have trouble meeting. He has told the voters that everything will be fine, that they will have tax cuts for three years running, that his programs will put people back to work, that the nation will once again enjoy abundant energy, balanced budgets, less government, more defense, and a halt to rampant inflation — all without sacrifice by the American people.

His major endeavors require time. But the public is impatient, and the first crucial tests of his leadership will fall upon him quickly.

Four years ago, Jimmy Carter sowed the seeds of several major failures and disappointments in the first 100 days of his administration. He had run as an outsider and instead of immediately forging a governing coalition with Congressional Democrats, he set Congress on edge — and never really recovered — with his moralistic insistence on an early battle over water projects that powerful members of Congress felt impelled to protect. He ignored potential questions of propriety that would be raised against his friend Bert Lance, and later Lance's forced resignation bled the credibility of his own high-minded ethics. He embarked on economic policies that fed the fires of inflation which ultimately consumed him politically. He attempted an abrupt change of direction in arms talks with the Russians that cost precious time and ultimately helped delay an arms pact past the time when the Senate would accept it. He went too far in popularizing the Presidency and lost the aura of leadership.

The first 100 days of the new administration will test Reagan, too, and provide critical clues about his sureness of purpose, his flexibility, his tenacity, his judgment, his balance, his political touch.

Will he, for example, reach out to Democrats and moderate Republicans to broaden his governing coalition, or will he feel bound by loyalty to right-wing partisans? Will he pragmatically moderate his pronouncements and programs or hew to his most hard-line rhetoric of years past? Will he, like Carter, overload Congress in his initial enthusiasm and thus confound his own main objectives? Will the New Right lure him into debilitating skirmishes over school prayers, capital punishment, and abortion and distract him from the overarching economic and foreign policy priorities of the Presidency? Will Russian toughness or his own early stridency doom arms control? Will he be drawn, ill-prepared, into regional conflict abroad? Can he devise and pursue an effective anti-inflation program and gain public confidence for it?

In short, now that Reagan has won the opportunity to prove that conservativism works, what kind of leadership will he provide? Will he be able to raise the American standard of living and national self-esteem sufficiently over the next four years so that in the presidential debates of 1984 no Democrat dares pose to voters the question that Reagan used so effectively against President Carter: "Are you better off today than you were four years ago?"

The challenge before Reagan now is to insure that the next time that question is asked in earnest, the answer is yes.

I

A Star Is Born

Adam Clymer

Ronald Reagan set foot on the national political stage on October 27, 1964, when he made a half-hour televised speech for the Republican presidential candidate, Barry Goldwater. It did not draw much critical attention. That was long before newspapers seriously covered the role of television in politics, and neither *The New York Times* nor *The Los Angeles Times* mentioned the speech. Neither did Theodore H. White in his *The Making of the President 1964*. That collective inattention may hardly be surprising, for in the politics of that year the speech was ineffective. It did nothing to avert electoral disaster for Goldwater, a disaster that left his ideological allies on the defensive for many years.

But 27,178,188 Americans voted for Barry Goldwater in 1964, and a sizable fraction of them heard and watched Reagan. His speech articulated and renewed the hopes that Goldwater's impending defeat had dulled. So, instead of despairing one week later on Election Day, they stayed in the politics that many had entered only to help Goldwater. Twelve and sixteen years later, many of them were running Reagan-for-President headquarters,

7

like Diana Evans in Portland, Oregon, and telling reporters they were with Reagan because "he simply talks common sense." For her, and for millions of others, the 1964 Reagan speech was the political equivalent of his most famous moment in the movies, when, as a mortally ill football star, George Gipp, he told coach Knute Rockne from his deathbed, "Rock, some day when the team is up against it and the breaks are beating the boys, ask 'em to go in there with all they've got and win just one for the Gipper. I don't know where I'll be then, but I'll know about it. I'll be happy." Some day they would be ready to win just one, not for the Gipper and Notre Dame, but for Reagan and the Republicans.

The 1964 speech itself did not praise Goldwater or denounce President Lyndon Johnson. Instead it argued the conservative cause. It had one-liners that Reagan audiences would hear well into the 1980 campaign, lines like, "A government agency is the nearest thing to eternal life we'll ever see on this earth." It was studded with examples of the foolishness of the bureaucracy, like this account: "There are now two and a half million Federal employees. No one knows what they all do. One Congressman found out what one of them does. This man sits at a desk in Washington. Documents come to him each morning. He reads them, initials them, and passes them on to the proper agency. One day a document arrived that he wasn't supposed to read, but he read it, initialled it, and passed it on. Twenty-four hours later it arrived back at his desk with a memo attached that said, 'You weren't supposed to read this. Erase your initials, and initial the erasure.' "

That anecdotal style, even though from time to time reporters would go to work and prove the example a phony — as they often disproved Reagan's statistics — was brilliantly effective on the banquet circuit and on the stump. It is an absolutely essential part of Reagan's ability to make problems seem simple.

But the greatest strength of the speech was its inspirational tone. He equated the conservative struggle against bureaucracy with the international contest with Communism, and said that, at home, "The guns are silent in this war, but frontiers fall while those who should be warriors prefer neutrality."

"Not too long ago," he continued, "two friends of mine were talking to a Cuban refugee. He was a businessman who had escaped from Castro. In the midst of his tale of horrible experiences, one of my friends turned to the other and said, 'We don't know how lucky we are.' The Cuban stopped and said, 'How lucky you are? *I* had some place to escape to.' And in that sentence he told the entire story. If freedom is lost here there is no place to escape to."

Twenty-seven minutes later, after touching only lightly on foreign policy but cataloguing the domestic failings of the Federal government from TVA to Social Security to Federal Housing programs to tax policy, he told his audience: "You and I have a rendezvous with destiny. We can preserve for our children this last best hope of man on earth, or we can sentence them to take the first step into a thousand years of darkness. If we fail, at least let our children and our children's children say of us we justified our brief moment here. We did all that could be done."

But if the speech demonstrated the strengths that Reagan could bring to a political career, it reflected some of the weaknesses, too. Indeed, some Goldwater campaign officials tried to keep him from giving it on national television, although its earlier showings in California had proved a great fund-raising success. Their objection was to a passage in which he reopened one already painful wound of the Goldwater campaign, the subject of Social Security. He made perfectly acceptable complaints about the financial soundness of the Social Security system, but went on, in words that would be used against him in his 1980 campaign, to ask: "Can't we introduce voluntary features so that those who can make better provision for themselves are allowed to do so? Incidentally, we might also allow participants in Social Security to name their own beneficiaries, which they cannot do in the present program. These are not insurmountable problems."

That same insistence on pursuing politically lost causes turned up most dramatically in the summer of 1980, when Reagan would not give up on the subject of Taiwan, a dead issue if there ever was one, until he brought it up and made his own judgment, not

REAGAN THE MAN, THE PRESIDENT

on the status of the island, a live question. One of his oldest political friends, reflecting on that issue, recalled that he once had a dog named Sam that could not be trained out of hunting porcupines, no matter how many times he came whimpering to have the quills pulled out of his nose. When Reagan gets fixed on an issue, like Society Security in 1964 or Taiwan in 1980, said the friend, "he's tenacious as hell," and, like Sam, he "gets his snout in the path of the porcupine."

The Goldwater aides, and even the Senator himself, failed to talk Reagan out of giving the speech, and the campaign's television arm put it on the air twice, raising something like $1 million. But no one will ever know the exact amount raised, according to F. Clifton White, an important Goldwater operative that year, because "I had people calling me to get prints and putting it on locally. In Denver it ran three or four times." Every local showing raised more money.

Reagan, who had brushed aside approaches that he run for office, first from Democrats in the 1940s and then from his new party (he actually changed his registration in 1962) in 1962 and 1964, made it clear he expected an active role in Republican politics. He began the day after the Election by attacking Republicans who had deserted Goldwater, approvingly quoting the Arizona Senator, who said, "You can't win an election and fight your own party." But that commentary was mild compared with what Reagan told Los Angeles Young Republicans a week later: "We don't intend to turn the Republican Party over to the traitors in the battle just ended." He scoffed at non-Goldwater Republicans, saying, "We will have no more of those candidates who are pledged to use the same socialist goals of our opposition."

Some of his friends thought they knew where to find a candidate without any tendency at all toward socialist goals. Holmes Tuttle, an automobile dealer and entrepreneur who had known Reagan eighteen years at that point, described their thinking this way: "After we took that terrible defeat in 1964, we knew we had to do something. We sat down and licked our wounds for a while, but we knew he'd already been accepted as being in the arena of politics because of the speech." So Tuttle and others went to Reagan in early 1965, urging him to run for Governor of California.

Tuttle and others, like Henry Salvatori, an oil developer, kept urging Reagan to run. The success of his friend George Murphy in that year's Senate race made it clear that being a former movie actor was no disqualification, something his opponents found to their dismay when their campaign commercials making fun of his movie roles backfired in 1966. But Reagan again demurred. Finally Tuttle went to Reagan's home again and changed tactics, not asking him to run but asking him to let Tuttle and others explore the possibilities.

Reagan agreed, probably without deciding if he really wanted to run for Governor, establishing a manner of making political decisions by one early move. This was to be his pattern in 1968 and 1976 as well. Friends of Ronald Reagan, an organization created by Bill Roberts and Stuart Spencer, the ace California political managers, started drumming up support, and Reagan, after assuring them he was not going to run an ideological campaign, decided to run by September of 1965.

It turned out to be a surprisingly easy campaign, both in the primary and the general election. The Democrats were overconfident, and Californians had tired of Edmund G. (Pat) Brown as Governor after eight years in office. Reagan did not worry about the movie star issue and surrounded himself on the campaign trail with actors like Andy Devine, Chuck Connors, and Edgar Bergen. With little to worry about financially, the Reagan staff expanded, and he won a relatively mild primary campaign by an overwhelming margin over George Christopher, the former Mayor of San Francisco.

In 1980, when the candidate was sixty-nine years old, reporters sometimes ridiculed his light pace of campaigning, but even in 1966, at fifty-five, he often managed a nap in the afternoon. There was less to note in the success of the Reagan campaign than in the failures of Democratic attacks against him. They thought they could label him as an extremist, naming him as a front man for the John Birch Society. They counted on the movie background to

11

work against him, and it did not. They counted on Reagan to say something disastrously stupid, and he didn't. The same expectations failed Jimmy Carter fourteen years later.

Reagan won the Governorship by 993,739 votes, and it wasn't long before his friends were thinking big. In fact, Tuttle concedes that they had the White House in mind even before Reagan went to Sacramento. "It didn't take a real smart man to know that we had a viable candidate for Governor, and if he did a good job he would be presidential timber," Tuttle recalled in his modest Los Angeles office near the automobile dealership he owns. They were talking about how to bring it off as early as February 1967, but it is anything but clear how firmly Reagan himself ever was committed to a 1968 presidential candidacy. William French Smith, a Los Angeles lawyer who is among Reagan's intimates, and was then, insists, "When he moved to Sacramento in 1967, the press started talking about him as being a future presidential possibility. At that time he certainly had no such thought himself. He was too occupied in the job he was just starting to do."

As Smith recalls it, Reagan then was less seized with ambition for the Presidency than he was pleased that here he was, barely in his first public office, and columnists and conservative Republicans were talking about him as a presidential possibility. "It's very flattering to be wanted for President of the United States," Smith observed.

Reagan, who in his 1966 campaign had pledged to serve out his four-year gubernatorial term, was coy about the efforts made to help him. "There's not much I can do about it," he said as late as mid-April 1968. That was so much traditional political hokum. He could have stopped it, and he didn't. Late in 1967, Tom Reed, one of his closest aides, left the Governor's staff to work on the 1968 presidential candidacy, and hired film-makers to produce material that could substitute for the noncampaigning noncandidate. Lyn Nofziger, Reagan's press secretary, checked the material over, too, although Reagan himself kept up his pretense on noninvolvement by not looking at any of the material, until curiosity overtook him just before the Oregon primary that May.

But the major step that Salvatori, Tuttle, and the others took — the one that gave the effort professional credibility — was the hiring of Cliff White. Technically his role was that of "adviser to the California delegation." That delegation was pledged to Reagan as their "favorite son," and no one moved into the state to take him on. But White was obviously promoting a real candidacy, though the task was much trickier than it had been when he went out early — before 1964 — for Goldwater, hitting one state capital after another.

White looks back on that ultimately unsuccessful effort with amusement. His overwhelming obstacle was the inability to present Reagan to potential supporters as a real, live candidate. "Californians think anyone they have elected Governor already has the highest honor in the land, and so there was great nervousness about the California reaction if he ran for President." So White had to settle for saying he thought Reagan would run, a very unsatisfactory way to sell a candidate.

An even greater obstacle was that this time White was up against the forces of Richard Nixon. If Reagan had raised $1.5 million for Republican Party organs in 1967, Nixon had raised several times that over much more than a decade. In 1966 Nixon had traveled almost constantly to help Republican candidates for Congress, and a great many of them gave him credit for their successes. In Reagan's area of greatest strength, the South, Nixon was well-connected and popular. The Nixon campaign was sewing up delegates while the Reagan forces were still plotting. And in the one state where Tom Reed and his colleagues made a serious effort, Oregon, Nelson Rockefeller won the primary with the slogan "He cared enough to come." Reagan, still the noncandidate, did not cross California's northern border, and only got 23 percent of the vote. (He was on the ballot because the Secretary of State put him there, under state law which requires serious potential candidates to be listed.)

An increasing, and thus increasingly obvious, level of political speaking that spring led up to the Miami Beach Republican convention itself, where Reagan formally announced his candidacy and rattled the Nixon forces badly. Reagan's supporters were able to do it with the help of the fundamentally improbable alliances of American politics, a working arrangement to share information on delegates with the Rockefeller campaign organization. Their candidate, of course, also had to see Nixon stopped before he could hope to win the nomination.

What White had been able to obtain, in seven hard months of working the delegates, was a handsome number of pledges of support on a second ballot. (Every four years memories, or legends, of multiballot conventions are dusted off in the political press, but the last time the Democrats took more than one ballot to pick their nominee was 1952, and the Republicans have also not gone beyond a first ballot since that year.) And that had the Nixon forces worried, in part because they had felt that deals with Southern party leaders had guaranteed them delegate support, which some of their friends among Southern Republicans were finding hard to hold for the former Vice-President. On Monday night, two days before the crucial first ballot, CBS News broadcast the first serious delegate count since Reagan's formal declaration of candidacy that afternoon, and it found Nixon with 626, or forty-one short of a majority, Rockefeller at 243, Reagan at 192 (but moving up), and favorite sons and others with the remaining 272.

Reagan worked one delegation after another, but found that prospective allies like Senator Strom Thurmond of South Carolina and even Goldwater were working Nixon's side of the street. They got assorted commitments Nixon would rather not have had, especially Thurmond, who was able to present himself as though he had a veto over Nixon's vice-presidential choice. In the end, but by only twenty-five votes, Nixon had his first-ballot majority.

Cliff White, in 1980 an enthusiastic Reagan adviser, reminisced one day at the campaign headquarters in Arlington about his 1968 efforts. He remembered two things in particular. The first was that in 1968, when White would drop in at the Governor's office to report how things were going, "every once in a while, he would say, 'Hey, I've decided to go back to the ranch.' "

Second, an impression that "Ronald Reagan really looks upon

public office as public service, and he has the high school senior's attitude that you do what you're expected to do, but you're not supposed to vote for yourself."

But that 1968 Reagan, jokingly diffident about the highest office in the land, and reluctant to push himself too hard, was not the 1976 Reagan. After six more years in Sacramento (his 1970 second-term majority was only half as big, but it was still comfortable), satisfied that he had done a good job running the government of the largest state in the Union (even his critics agreed that he had not been as bad a Governor as he had threatened to be), Reagan approached 1976 in a very different position.

First of all, he had expected Richard Nixon to serve out his term. Then Reagan had planned to take on all comers, especially Vice-President Spiro T. Agnew, for the nomination — and to win. But a funny thing happened on that road to the White House: Mr. Nixon resigned his office before he could be impeached, and suddenly there was an incumbent Republican President, eligible for another term, to run against.

That made a difference. Reagan had some very serious reservations about running against an incumbent of his own party. The "Eleventh Commandment" — a motto of California Republican politics enunciated by a former state Republican chairman, Gaylord Parkinson — had served Reagan well in deflecting George Christopher's attacks on him as inexperienced in 1966, and Reagan was reluctant to violate its precept: "Thou Shalt Not Speak Ill of Other Republicans."

But while Reagan is a Republican of fixed principles, whose political philosophy really changes only through slight shifts of emphasis, not through fundamental reversals, he is not a traditional politician. William French Smith argues that Reagan does not have "a lack of respect for tradition" — although to run against President Gerald R. Ford for the 1976 nomination was plainly that. But Smith does not disagree with the account of John P. Sears, Reagan's campaign manager until he was dumped in February 1980. "If you come to him with a different idea," said Sears, who often did just that, "he never told you, 'Things just aren't done that way.' He asked you to explain, and if your idea was convincing, he would buy it."

The decision to run in 1975, despite the Ford incumbency, was not all that different from the decision to run for Governor of California in 1965. Eventually, after discussions upon discussions, Reagan consented to the formation of an "exploratory committee," one of those tedious fictions of American politics. Such committees almost never return without reporting that they have sighted a presidential nomination out there in the wilderness. When he agreed to the formation of the committee in midsummer, he foreordained the announcement of his candidacy in November.

Reagan's 1975-1976 campaign for the nomination was the first real run at an incumbent Republican President, within his party, since Theodore Roosevelt's bid in 1912. It was well thought-out, in tactical terms, though not always well executed. Some state filing deadlines passed because the campaign headquarters was preoccupied with other problems. John Sears was a master tactician, whose own popularity with the press, and skill in handling reporters, gave the campaign a major boost in credibility. But the campaign staff, though talented, was not deep, and it tended to concentrate more upon tactics than issues, while Reagan assumed they were watching all his flanks.

The major problem on the issues in his 1976 campaign was created by a speech he gave in September 1975, a speech the campaign high command had looked over, but not very carefully. In it he proposed getting the Federal government out of $90 billion worth of social programs, from welfare to education. When he got to New Hampshire for his first serious campaigning the next January, the Ford campaign was waiting for him, with detailed charges about how the cost of replacing Federal services would require that low-tax state to enact an income tax, or a sales tax, or both. Reagan explained and explained, talking about transferring the revenue from Federal liquor and cigarette taxes, or perhaps a share of what a state's residents paid in income taxes, to the states to make up the gap. Reagan contends to this day that the idea helped his campaign. But everybody else in his campaign and out of it thinks that the defensive position he was forced to adopt slowed his momentum and contributed to his narrow loss in the New Hampshire primary — a state many outsiders had thought he would win.

New Hampshire in February was followed quickly by defeats in Massachusetts, Florida, and Illinois, and the latter two states had, in the early flush of the campaign, seemed ripe for Reagan. The campaign was nearly broke, and there was talk of dropping out. It bothered Reagan, and the Eleventh Commandment began to lose its authority for him. Complaining about how Ford would distribute Federal grants as he campaigned, Reagan charged, "The band doesn't know whether to play 'Hail to the Chief' or 'Santa Claus Is Coming to Town.' "

But the device that made a difference was the use of Reagan, speaking into the camera, for thirty minutes on television all over the state. Reagan says it was his idea to make the tape, when a Florida station decided it owed him thirty minutes of equal time. "Everyone said, 'How are we going to use this time?' " he recalled in an interview not long after. "I said, 'I'll use it, giving my basic speech.' " It made little difference in one Florida showing, but it worked in North Carolina, where Reagan scored an upset win, and then a new version was shown nationally and raised enough money to keep the campaign going until the more hospitable Texas primary on May 1.

No matter who came up with the tactic, it was unconventional and against the advice of the professionals who were making Reagan's rather flat commercials. And so, for the second time in his career, a straight-on televised speech played a vital role in his career.

In Texas, where Reagan's conservatism, and especially his Panama Canal formula ("We built it, we paid for it, it's ours, and we're going to keep it.") played better than country music, Reagan profited by the fact that both Lloyd Bentsen, a Texas Senator, and Governor George C. Wallace of Alabama were no longer serious

Democratic candidates. Jimmy Carter was almost all alone in his party's primary, so conservatives had no serious contest to vote in except the Republican primary.

When the results came in late that Saturday night, Reagan had shut out Ford, winning all ninety-six delegates at stake. He followed that victory three days later with triumphs in Georgia, Alabama, and Indiana. Meanwhile Reagan was doing well in caucuses and conventions in the Mountain states, and it was a real contest.

But Ford made a comeback, too, and won in Michigan and Ohio, in two crucial victories, coming out of the primaries with a slight lead in delegates. Neither candidate had enough to win, but Ford was closer. And if there ever was an occasion when the power of the White House helped in a political campaign, this was it. Ford was winning over uncommitted delegates every day, closing in on the majority needed for nomination in Kansas City. Reagan's telephone calls to the waverers were no match for calls in which a White House operator would announce, "The President is calling." And when he called there were invitations to the White House, even invitations to view the Bicentennial spectacle of the Tall Ships in New York harbor from the deck of the same aircraft carrier where Ford would watch them pass in review.

So when Sears came to Reagan with another unusual idea, Reagan was receptive, even though it had never been done before. Speculation over who will be chosen as a vice-presidential candidate usually continues until the nominee himself is picked, and formally nominated. But Sears suggested they pick someone, right then in mid-July, someone who might be able to appeal to uncommitted delegates in a region where Reagan himself was weak.

He suggested Senator Richard Schweiker of Pennsylvania, until then a Ford supporter, as someone who might attract delegates in his own state and perhaps New York. Reagan listened for about twenty minutes, and then asked Sears several questions about how it would be done, but none, according to Sears, that questioned the wisdom of doing something that had not been done before. Then he called Senator Paul Laxalt of Nevada, an old friend who had been Governor of his state when Reagan was in Sacramento. Laxalt was Schweiker's seatmate in the Senate, and Reagan wanted to know if he was basically a conservative. Laxalt said he was, so Reagan agreed to see the Pennsylvanian.

It was an intensely controversial move, which led Southern conservatives to an undying hatred for Sears. It was a bold gamble that did not work, but it worked no less well than standing pat would have worked. Schweiker attracted no additional delegates to speak of, and Reagan's own campaigning (including an odd, tentative offer to send American troops to Rhodesia) won few more. It was left to Sears to try some adventures with convention rules that he hoped would force Ford to name a running mate, too, and thus lose either liberal or conservative support. But, though Reagan forces won a series of platform fights, they went down solidly to defeat at the convention, never approaching the breakthrough needed for nomination.

After Ford won and gave a tough, enthusiastic acceptance speech, he called Reagan up to the podium, and Reagan gave a brief talk that outshone Ford's, once again, as in the 1964 speech, cheering the defeated Republican right on to fight another day.

He praised Ford, but most of all he praised the Republican platform. "There are cynics who say that a party platform is something that no one bothers to read, and it doesn't very often amount to much." But this time, he said, "The Republican Party has a platform that is a banner of bold unmistakable colors with no pale pastel shades." He talked of Americans a hundred years hence, and said, "Whether they have the freedom that we have known up until now will depend on what we do here. Will they look back with appreciation and say, 'Thank God for those people in 1976 who headed off that loss of freedom, who kept us now a hundred years later free, who kept our world from nuclear destruction?'

"This is our challenge. And this is why, here in this hall to-night, better than we've ever done before, we've got to quit talking to each other and about each other and go out and communicate to the world that we may be fewer in numbers than we've ever been, but we carry the message they're waiting for. We must go

19

forth from here united, determined, believing what a great general said a few years ago. 'There is no substitute for victory.' "

Reagan, of course, was quoting General Douglas MacArthur's famous 1951 farewell address to Congress, the speech that concluded, "Old soldiers never die; they just fade away. I now close my military career and just fade away."

Ronald Reagan did not follow MacArthur's example.

II

Creating the Role

Robert Lindsey

It often seems that American Presidents come out of regional offices of Central Casting: If Jimmy Carter's Georgia accent and demeanor frequently seemed to remind Americans of some of their clichés about the rural South; John Kennedy's urbane humor, voice, and style seemed to fit their preconceptions about upper crust Boston; Lyndon Johnson was almost a caricature cowboy of Texas, big, masculine, and sometimes vulgar; Richard Nixon suggested a nouveau riche California, slightly insecure, on the make, and as trustworthy as a Los Angeles car dealer, some critics would say. Ronald Reagan represents other sides to some of those clichés upon which people have built their images of California; he was the handsome movie star, an immigrant from Middle America, like millions of other Californians who came west during the 1930s to seek their fortunes and brought with them small-town conservative Middle Western values.

Ronald Reagan is by profession a performer, and it is the single most important fact about him. He is a consummate performer who trained to be Governor of the nation's most populous state and trained for the Presidency by perfecting his skills as an actor and communicator in the movies and on television and before thousands of audiences as General Electric's traveling salesman on the virtues of the free enterprise system. His greatest single skill is his ability to communicate an idea or an emotion.

Reagan strides onto a stage with the confidence of a man who's been on one, listening to applause, for the better part of forty-five years. Balloons rise into the air, the audience, as often as not, jumps to its feet, and a band strikes up, "California Here I Come." Confident and smiling, waving his hands and waiting while the applause begins to subside, Reagan is never more in his element than when he is standing before such an audience, especially in Small-Town America, telling it what it wants to hear. With timing honed in thousands of such appearances, he campaigns with a message that seldom varies from the simple values of his old General Electric speech.

Reeling off a litany of statistics and one-liner jokes, he assails the Democrats who, he says, have, in effect, given up on the American Dream by telling Americans that they must prepare for a future with less energy, less material abundance, less opportunity for the next generation.

He assails the Russians, as bent as ever, he says, on a Communist takeover of the world, and warns darkly of the decline of American military might, which once dominated the world but no longer does; and, again, he deplores the oppression of ordinary Americans by profligate, tax-greedy Big Government.

He rails at how General Motors must employ more than 20,000 employees just to fill out government forms, and says one agency of government alone processes enough paper each year to "cover the District of Columbia three times over. . . ."

He pauses a moment or two and then adds, "And maybe that's not a bad idea. . . ."

When he was growing up, Reagan recalls, a young man or woman had boundless opportunities to get ahead. But now the incentive of individuals and business has been stifled by high taxes and government regulators. Let's free the oil industry from government regulation, he says, and the oil companies will solve the energy crisis; hasn't American ingenuity and drive always solved the country's problems?

"Jimmy Carter said we should give back the Panama Canal because nobody would like us if we didn't. . . . Jimmy Carter says we should sign the SALT II treaty because nobody will like us if we don't. . . .

"Well, I say, isn't it about time we stopped worrying about whether people like us and say, 'We want to be respected again!' "

From the rural backwoods of New England to the farm towns of the Middle West, from the suburbs of Los Angeles to the retirement villages of Arizona and Florida, audiences heard these words during the 1980 presidential campaign and, as if propelled from their seats by the same electric shock, rose to their feet and exploded into long and emotional applause.

In truth, Jimmy Carter never said America should return the Canal to Panama — or sign the SALT II treaty — because nobody would like the United States if it didn't. But, it didn't matter. Reagan's audiences clearly longed for a leader who felt as they did, who felt the same gnawing feeling in his stomach, the same uncomfortable sense of insecurity and the end of confidence in Americans and their country. But more, he was an orator who convinced them that it didn't have to be that way, that he knew how to turn back the clock and restore the United States to the un-rivaled position of power it once had in the world, who could make them believe, as he often said, that America, since its earliest days, had been a "nation of destiny" and that it could become a land of opportunity again, where, if you played by the rules, you could get ahead, maybe even get rich.

Ronald Reagan was a member of a generation of Hollywood actors and actresses who were bound by contracts to powerful studios that churned out movies as if they were operating an assembly line; a handful of moguls ran the studios like medieval fiefdoms, rigidly controlling the flow of films to an eager audience, as well as the careers of their players, few of whom risked the wrath of the moguls for fear of losing their privileged position. The contract players acted on demand, reading lines written by contract writers and directed by contract directors, rarely being given a choice of the roles they played or a chance to play in a truly distinguished movie, aware that for every *Gone With the Wind* there were a hundred lesser films.

It was from this professional milieu that Ronald Reagan would begin his political career, and it helped make him perhaps the most effective American political orator since Franklin Delano Roosevelt, who, espousing virtually everything that Reagan would later denounce, was, curiously, his childhood idol and the model for his own oratorical style.

Yet Reagan did more than master the skills of oratory. From his roots in the heartland of the nation during the lean years of the Depression and later, during and after World War II, he evolved a personal set of beliefs, of what some pundits, not always approvingly, called "traditional" values — belief in God and the family, America right-or-wrong patriotism, optimism about the future, and the conviction that hard work will bring its rewards. In later years, he would be accused time and again of being simplistic and demagogic as he toured the country saying, or so it seemed, that the solution to virtually all of the nation's problems was to get government out of people's hair.

Still, earlier than any other major American politician, he recognized a tide of conservatism that would affect much of the country during the later 1970s. He became the spokesman for a kind of populist conservatism rooted in some of the same values that he brought with him to California in the late 1930s. Another Republican, Barry Goldwater, would in 1964 offer American voters many of the same values, but Reagan's timing was different; more important, he was more effective in getting his message across to the voters. He was a better after-dinner speaker.

Ronald Wilson Reagan was born in Tampico, Illinois, on February 6, 1911, in a small flat above the H.C. Pitney General Store, where his father sold shoes. Reagan wrote in his 1966 autobiography that, according to reports, "My face was blue from screaming, my bottom was red from whacking, and my father claimed afterward that he was white when he said, 'For such a little bit of a fat Dutchman, he makes a hell of a lot of noise, doesn't he?' Ever since my birth my nickname has been 'Dutch,' and I have been particularly fond of the colors that were exhibited — red, white and blue."

Some youngsters who grow up in Middle Western hamlets like Tampico, Illinois (population 1,200), deplore their isolation and lack of big city distractions, but Reagan didn't — or at least he didn't in hindsight, when he recalled his youth in his autobiography. "My existence turned into one of those rare Huck Finn-Tom Sawyer idylls," he wrote of growing up in Tampico, with "woods and mysteries, life and death among the small creatures, hunting and fishing." They were, he wrote, "the happiest times of my life." It wasn't an especially easy life; his father drank a good deal — "He had the Irish disease," Ronald Reagan would say many years later — and sometimes found it difficult to keep a job. But John Edward Reagan, a first generation "black Irishman," was nevertheless an ambitious man and the family frequently moved as he sought a better job. By all accounts he and his wife, Nellie, presided over a family that was warm and close-knit.

From his mother, who coached a local dramatic group, Reagan got his first taste of acting; his father, on the other hand, provided the earliest influence on his political outlook. Jack Reagan was a hard worker who, much of his life, longed to own his own store, and he eventually became part owner of one in Dixon, Illinois, in 1920. The older man's dreams of owning his own store, and his eventual achievement of the dream, if only briefly (he lost the store, financed on borrowed money, during the Depression), may help explain Ronald Reagan's later close affinity with entrepreneurs who provided much of his financial support during his early bids for political office.

Reagan, in his autobiography, *Where's the Rest of Me?*, called his father "a sentimental Democrat who believed fervently about the battle at Herrin in 1922, where twenty-six persons were killed in a massacre brought about by a coal mine strike — he never lost his conviction that the individual must stand on his own feet. . . ."

He believed literally that all men were created equal and that the man's own ambition determined what happened to him after that . . . ," Reagan wrote about his father. This would become one of the cornerstones of Reagan's own philosophy, a seminal inspiration for his standard General Electric speech.

His father figures in another part of the Reagan oratorical literature, in an account of how he and his brother came home from college during the Christmas holidays in 1931 just in time to see his father receive, instead of a Christmas bonus, a "blue slip" announcing that he had been fired. It is a story that Reagan always tells emotionally and one that older members of his audience respond to. Like his father, Ronald Reagan became a devoted supporter of Franklin D. Roosevelt after his election in 1932, enthusiastic, like his father, for the reforms of the New Deal designed to pull the country out of the Depression. Along with others in his family, he sat around the radio listening to Roosevelt's "Fireside Chats" and would later say that he had patterned part of his own speaking style and televised appeals to California voters after FDR's methods. Besides his father, the most important influence in shaping Reagan's early outlook on life was his brother, Neil, who was two years older, and to whom he often turned for advice as a child.

Reagan's earliest success was modest; in high school he gained prominence playing football and other sports. He worked summers and on weekends as a lifeguard and in other jobs, and, at seventeen, went away to Eureka College, a morally conservative institution run by the Disciples of Christ. He plunged deeply into student activities and sports but would have a markedly undistinguished academic record and, indeed, would often say later that his intellectual experience at college was far less important to him than his more satisfying experiences in sports, drama, and other student activities. During his frustrations as Governor in dealing with campus radicals at the University of California in the 1960s, his critics would find irony in the fact that he had helped lead a student strike that led to the resignation, under pressure, of the college's puritanical president.

He graduated from Eureka in 1932 at the depth of the Depression, bitten by a bug to enter show business and uncertain how to go about it. "Broadway and Hollywood were as inaccessible as outer space," he recalled later in his autobiography. He decided that for a young college graduate in Illinois his best avenue to achieve fame and a possible eventual bid from Hollywood or Broadway was radio, and he succeeded in landing a job in Davenport, Iowa, at station WOC (the initials stand for World of Chiropractic, an indirect tribute to Colonel B.L. Palmer of the Palmer School of Chiropractic, who founded the station). On WOC and later on a sister station, WHO in Des Moines, Iowa, Reagan began to excell at a new art form — broadcasting play-by-play descriptions of baseball games that he didn't attend, but pretended to, by reconstructing the events from Western Union reports of each play. Dutch Reagan, talkative, persuasive, and gifted with a voice and demeanor that gave him credibility, was soon one of the best known play-by-play announcers in the Middle West, and when he wasn't on the radio, he found himself in growing demand to give speeches to local clubs and other organizations.

He still had his ambitions for bigger things, though, and in 1937, while he accompanied the Chicago Cubs on a trip to southern California for spring training, he looked up a friend who had contacts in the Hollywood studios. Reagan, who is nearsighted (he now wears contact lenses), was advised to take off his glasses for the interview and screen test that followed. Within a few days, he had a contract with Warner Brothers.

In subsequent years, political adversaries depicted Reagan as a "second rate actor in B pictures" or "the nice guy who never got the girl." It is true from a retrospective look at Reagan's films that he did not possess some of the qualities that elevated some of his contemporaries and competitors, such as Gary Cooper, Clark Gable, Robert Taylor, or Errol Flynn, to superstardom. Nevertheless, it is equally clear that until his career was sidetracked by World War II, and, to an extent, by his own post-war obsession with the Screen Actors Guild, Reagan had a more than successful film career and delivered several portrayals that earned him laudatory notices from the critics, especially in *Brother Rat; Knute Rockne, All-American; Dark Victory;* and *King's Row.*

He made fifty-one pictures in all, and, contrary to what his political enemies said, he often got the girl. Given the conditions under which he worked, it is probably noteworthy that any of the pictures were memorable. After his debut, playing a radio announcer in *Love Is on the Air,* he made seven other pictures for Warner Brothers during his first eleven months in Hollywood. The same pace continued after the first year, and he frequently found himself shifting from one picture to the next month after month. In Hollywood, he had a reputation as a reliable journeyman, a second-level matinee idol with a handsome face and boy-next-door appeal, who learned his lines and was rarely late to work. There wasn't much time for quality under the old Hollywood factory system. He wrote, "They didn't want it good; they wanted it Thursday."

Before long, Reagan felt his career was well enough established to bring his parents to Los Angeles, and he bought them their first home; after a while, his brother came, too, to begin a successful advertising career in California.

Reagan dated young starlets with enough frequency to be mentioned often in the gossip columns, but had a reputation as a social conservative in a town where many film stars felt they had a franchise to live on their own terms with society's mores. In 1939, while making *Brother Rat,* he began a courtship with one of his costars, Jane Wyman, and on January 25, 1940, they were married in Hollywood, with his parents looking on.

In 1942, Reagan gave what most film writers have described as his best performance, in *King's Row.* He played Drake McCugh, a young man injured in a car accident, who is treated by a physician who had objected to McCugh dating his daughter. In a kind of perverted revenge, the physician amputates the young man's legs, prompting Reagan, when he discovers they are gone, to speak his most famous line — "Where is the rest of me?" the title of his autobiography.

Before leaving Iowa, Reagan had joined the Army cavalry as a reserve officer, and he was activated after Pearl Harbor. But, because of his poor eyesight, he was given "limited duty," which meant he was assigned to a unit making training films for the Army Air Corps. Situated not far from the MGM studios in Culver City, the unit was called by some of its members, including stars such as Alan Ladd, the "Culver City Commandos" and "Fort Wacky." On occasion, he noted in his autobiography, it undertook projects that were vital to the war effort. "Possibly our most important job was also our most secret — in fact, it was one of the better kept secrets of the war, ranking up with the atom bomb project. . . .

"All on our own, our special effects men — Hollywood geniuses in uniform — built a complete miniature of Tokyo. It covered most of the floor space of a sound stage; above this they rigged a crane and camera mount and could photograph the miniature, giving an effect on the screen of movies taken from a plane traveling at any prescribed height and speed."

When Army Air Corps generals heard about the project, Reagan wrote, they were dubious and sent a delegation to inspect a film simulating flight over Tokyo that was made using the technique. "Skepticism turned to enthusiasm," Reagan recalled, saying that the military officers concluded that the technique offered an otherwise unavailable means to give pilots a dress rehearsal before they bombed Tokyo.

When the war ended, a number of things had changed for Ronald Reagan. On the eve of Pearl Harbor, his career had been on the ascendant. He was getting better and better roles in films such as *King's Row,* he was earning more critical acclaim, and Warner Brothers had tripled his salary not long before he was placed on active military duty.

After the war, while he continued to make pictures, he never managed to recapture his career's pre-war momentum; with a few exceptions, he was relegated again to B pictures with poor scripts. "I had a sneaking suspicion that a lot of people across America hadn't stayed in a breathless state of palpitation for three and a half years waiting for my return. They had a new set of heroes," he wrote in *Where's the Rest of Me?*

The second thing that had changed was his marriage to Jane Wyman, which had begun to collapse.

Third, a metamorphosis was occurring in the political thinking of New Dealer Ronald Reagan that carried him from post-war membership in such liberal organizations as the Americans for Democratic Action and the United World Federalists to his decision in 1962 to become a Republican and his subsequent emergence as spokesman and eventual standard bearer for the conservative right.

In later years he sometimes exaggerated the political distance he traveled during his political transformation, trying to make a political virtue out of his change from New Dealer to conservative Republican.

In his autobiography he wrote that he had blindly joined "every organization I could find that would guarantee to save the world." In truth, he never moved nearly as far to the left as some members of the Hollywood community, who flirted with Communism, socialism, and various left-wing causes. He belonged briefly to one organization, the Hollywood Independent Committee of the Arts, Sciences and Professions, that was later accused of being a Communist front, and another, the American Veterans' Committee, that was suspected of Communist links, but in both cases he quit as soon as he discovered their orientation. Still, like many other Americans who had lived through World War II, he was gripped by a sense of idealism after the war that caused him to embrace liberal goals, such as increasing social equality and civil liberties, espoused by the Americans for Democratic Action and similar groups.

Reagan is a man who tends to chose his position on most issues on the basis of his own experiences rather than scholarly research. To a certain extent, he recalled later, the shift in his political outlook probably began while he was listening to his father and, especially, his brother describe excesses of the New Deal.

During the early thirties, all three of the Reagan males were strong New Deal Democrats, but toward the close of the decade Neil Reagan began to complain that Franklin D. Roosevelt had gone too far. Ronald Reagan later noted that he first began to be aware of what he considered the inefficiency and blunted incentives that result from an overgrown government while listening to his father talk about the Federal bureaucracy that had grown up around the W.P.A.; at one time, both worked for the Works Projects Administration. Neil Reagan had also become troubled by his inside look at government; he had become loosely affiliated with the Democratic machine in Chicago and told his brother that he was appalled by the corruption and patronage he witnessed and that he was thinking about leaving the Democratic Party. Ronald Reagan's antipathy was intensified, he said, during the war when he had his own first experiences with government efficiency: As the base personnel officer at Culver City, he wanted to lay off certain civilian employees who he felt were incompetent or unneeded. But he was prohibited from doing so by civil service regulations, and he didn't like it.

But it was probably Reagan's experience as a labor leader and his own increasing personal affluence as he grew older, as well as his subsequent role as spokesman for General Electric, that set him on the final course of his political evolution.

Reagan was recruited in 1938 to be a director for the Screen Actors Guild, a union formed five years earlier to give performers more clout in dealing with the all-powerful studios. After his release from the Army in 1945, he rejoined the board and was elected president of the union in 1947, remaining in this role until mid-1952; he was elected for another one-year term in 1959.

It was in some ways an ugly time for Hollywood, the era of the Communist witch hunt in which the House Committee on Un-American Activities was trying to uproot Communist sympathizers who, its members claimed, had used the power of the screen to further pro-Soviet propaganda. It was the time of the "black list," when writers and directors who had belonged to certain leftist groups or who had refused to answer some of the committee's questions were refused work in the film industry. It was also a time when there were indeed attempts by Communist-dominated labor unions and other organizations to influence the film industry, a powerful communications force in the United States.

Although the matter is still the subject of some debate in Hollywood, by most accounts Reagan acquitted himself honorably as a moderate during the film industry's crisis; he resisted what he called "unofficial blacklists," while leading an effective campaign against the relatively small but bona fide efforts of Communist organizations to grab power in the film community.

After an appearance before the House Committee on Un-American Activities in 1947, Reagan returned to Los Angeles to face another kind of crisis. The Hollywood gossip columns had already reported that the Ronald Reagan–Jane Wyman marriage was in trouble, and in February 1948 they separated. There was a brief, unsuccessful reconciliation, but that spring Miss Wyman told a Los Angeles judge that she could not continue the marriage. Her husband, she testified, had become so obsessed with the union and his political interests that there was no time left for her. "There was nothing in common between us, nothing to sustain our marriage," she said. Miss Wyman was awarded custody of their two children, Maureen and Michael.

While Reagan continued to devote more and more of his time to the Screen Actors Guild, he tried also to keep his film career alive, but, although he always seemed to be working on new films, they were, by and large, forgettable. Reagan was in some quarters becoming equally as well known for his role in the Screen Actors Guild as for his work as a leading man, and in 1952 he got a call from Mervyn LeRoy, the director, who asked him to do a favor for a young actress named Nancy Davis. The actress was troubled, LeRoy said, because her name frequently appeared on lists of Communist front organizations. "He guaranteed me that she was more than disinterested in leftist causes: she was violently opposed to such shenanigans."

Indeed she was. Reagan met the young actress and a courtship ensued. He learned that there were two Nancy Davises, and the other actress had joined what Reagan called the "bleeding heart" groups. Ronald Reagan had met a woman who not only shared his views that America faced a grave threat from Communism but agreed with him on just about everything else he said politically. Nancy Reagan would become the final important influence in shaping the thinking of Ronald Reagan before he began his missionary work for the General Electric Company. On March 4, 1952, they were married.

Many of the people who have watched the political ascendancy of Ronald Reagan say they believe that Nancy Reagan could be the single most important influence on him in the White House. From all appearances, they are extremely close, and Mrs. Reagan has become not only his wife but his political confidante, adviser, sounding board, and the person to whom he most often turns in trying to judge the motives and sincerity of people around him.

Although he discounts her role in shaping his conservative philosophy, their politics are practically indistinguishable. In her case, they largely reflect a background of affluence and security and the influence of her stepfather, Dr. Loyal Davis, a politically conservative Chicago surgeon, now retired. Dr. Davis married Mrs. Reagan's mother after her father, a New Jersey car salesman, had deserted the family when she was an infant, forcing her to be placed with relatives while her mother tried to support the family as an actress. Mrs. Reagan was adopted by Dr. Davis when she was fourteen.

She attended Girls Latin School in Chicago and Smith College and, encouraged by her mother, came to Hollywood during the 1940s, where she was one of thousands of other would-be starlets but was helped by the influence of Spencer Tracy and other friends of her parents who worked in the film industry. When she arrived at the Metro-Goldwyn-Mayer studios, she filled out a questionaire and, in response to a question on what her "greatest ambition" was, she said, "To have a successful happy marriage."

She was asked if she had any particular phobia and responded, "Superficiality. Vulgarity, especially in women. Untidiness of mind and person. And cigars."

She went on to appear in eleven movies, most of them undistinguished, including one, *Hellcats of the Navy,* in which she co-starred with her husband.

But this 1957 movie turned out to be the finale of her Hollywood career and she retired, in effect, to be Mrs. Ronald Reagan.

In Hollywood, she almost always played roles as sweet, feminine ingenues — an image that, in retrospect, she has maintained in her private life; she deplores many changes in modern morality, such as live-in relationships and premarital sex and abortion. It is a view of life that she shares with her husband and apparently was assimilated in her well-off, middle-class upbringing in Chicago.

Some people who have worked with Ronald Reagan have been critical of him as being overly reliant on others' opinions before making decisions and for having a tendency to take the advice of the last person who spoke to him on a particular problem. If this is true, Nancy Reagan could be the second most important person in the Reagan administration because she is the one in whom Reagan has the most confidence, according to people who know both of them.

Jim Lake, who served for many months as Reagan's press secretary during the 1980 campaign and was a close adviser, said: "They really have a storybook romance. The Governor really doesn't have bosom buddies in the normal sense that many men have, the kind he can go out and have a few drinks with and let his hair down with." The person he turns most to when he needs advice, Lake said, is his wife. "Nancy's his best friend."

III

California Rehearsal

Robert Lindsey

In Hollywood, if you didn't sing or dance, you would end up as an after-dinner speaker, so they made me an after-dinner speaker.   Ronald Reagan

Ronald Wilson Reagan, then fifty-five years old, was sworn in as Governor of California at sixteen minutes past midnight on January 2, 1967. The previous November he had beaten the Democratic incumbent, Edmund (Pat) Brown, the father of the man who would become Reagan's successor, by almost one million votes. With thirty-two television cameras focused on him, and looking as handsome and boyish as he did on a movie screen, Reagan glanced over at his old sidekick from Hollywood, United States Senator George Murphy, and quipped, "Well, here we are on the late show again."

For cynics around the country, the comment must have confirmed everything they thought about California. It was the ultimate California joke: two Hollywood celluloid celebrities, a politically inexperienced movie actor and a former song and dance man, now held two of the most important political offices in a state which, two years earlier, had overtaken New York to become the most populous in the nation. Many political professionals in California were just as cynical, and, in the state capitol at Sacramento, they waited for the man from Hollywood to begin doing his pratfalls.

Reagan had moved slowly, if unconsciously, from the role that first brought him to California, as a performer, to the fringes of political activism. He was earning a good living, not so much from acting, which he did with growing infrequency, but as a kind of professional after-dinner speaker, a traveling spokesman for the General Electric Company, one of his television sponsors. Reagan was given the job as part of a company public relations plan to enhance morale among employees in a corporation that was being increasingly decentralized, and he was personally encouraged by Ralph Cordiner, General Electric's board chairman. Reagan's message over the eight years he had the job became increasingly political. Drawing on his personal experiences in Hollywood, he assailed Communism, whose genuine dangers to the American way he felt were not adequately understood by most Americans, and gave a pep talk espousing the free enterprise system, which he felt was in jeopardy.

Whether he is delivering a speech or writing his autobiography, Reagan is fond of using numbers to make a point, and in *Where's the Rest of Me?*, in a passage that suggests the number of appearances during which he had a chance to polish his speaking style, the style that he said was inspired in part by FDR, he wrote of his years with General Electric: "I know statistics are boring, but reducing eight years of tours, in which I reached all the 135 plants and personally met with 250,000 employees down to numbers, it turns out something like this: two of the years were spent traveling and with speeches sometimes running at 14 a day, I was on my feet in front of a 'mike' for about 250,000 minutes."

Word of his talents as an after-dinner speaker on issues dear to the hearts of Republican conservatives had begun to spread in California. Early in 1964, Henry Salvatori would recall, "We invited Reagan to give a speech at one of our fund-raisers, and he was electrifying."

Long after he had himself become a professional politician, Reagan remained uneasy around most other political professionals, a calling that he often seemed to equate with the kind of Chicago ward heelers whom his brother had told him about years earlier. Instead, he preferred old friends from Hollywood or the company of successful businessmen, especially contemporaries like Holmes Tuttle, who had worked his way up from a Ford assembly line in his native Oklahoma to the prosperous ownership of five new-car dealerships and other businesses.

Tuttle and Reagan's other early backers were, for the most part, people like himself — middle-aged and older men who had come to California during the 1930s from the Middle West or the Dust Bowl without much money but with a great deal of ambition and had found success. Most of them, like his father, were entrepreneurs, but unlike his father, they had made it big. They regarded private enterprise as the secret of America's economic success and they objected when they saw a growing portion of the profits from their work disappear to finance a government that they felt was wasteful and inefficient, got into activities that rightfully belonged to the private entrepreneur, and encouraged people not to work.

"Every one of them is a self-made man," Tuttle once said of the group that became known as Reagan's "Millionaire Backers." In a discussion of why they had originally approached Reagan, he said: "We believed in the free enterprise system. We felt that if it was going to be preserved, instead of going around bellyaching about it we should go out and do something about it. We gathered people around who had a common interest and decided to help Ron."

California has a long if uneven tradition of accepting liberal political ideas, a tradition rooted partly in ugly scandals before the turn of the century, when the Southern Pacific Railroad ran the state almost as if it were a feudal duchy. The scandals helped set the stage for the election as Governor in 1910 of a Progressive

Party candidate, Hiram Johnson, who worked to clean up a corrupt Legislature and pushed for a number of liberal reforms, including giving Californians the right to amend the state constitution and bypass the Legislature by enacting their own laws through the initiative and referendum processes.

During the 1930s the state was tolerant enough to give author Upton Sinclair's leftish, utopian "End Poverty in California" movement a short-lived popularity. During the 1950s and 1960s under the administrations of Governors Earl Warren, Goodwin J. Knight, and Pat Brown, it built perhaps the best system of free public higher education in the world, a network of institutions that became not only incubators for new technologies and new industries, but the means for hundreds of thousands of young people from poor families to acquire a college degree. In later years, the environmental movement got its start in California.

But, along with a tradition of tolerance for new ideas, new politics, and new religions, there has also been a wary vein of conservatism in California, rooted perhaps in the relative newness of the state and the tenuous nature of success there. Unlike many states in the East, the Middle West, and the South, where family wealth and social status have often accrued over generations and are fairly secure, California, since the days of the Gold Rush, has been a state where people could start fresh and make it on their own, regardless of the social pecking order they came from. For some people, however, there can be a tentative quality to such success, a fear of losing it that breeds conservatism, insecurity, and pressure to maintain the status quo, and it can affect not only those who find great success like a Ronald Reagan or a Holmes Tuttle, but those whose success might be measured only by a good job, their own home, a car, a television set, and hopes of sending their children to college.

As Ronald Reagan would demonstrate in 1980, this kind of concern was not limited to California, but was felt by many blue-collar workers and other people all over the country. Many, deciding that what they had accumulated in life was threatened by inflation, changing moral attitudes, and a remote government that they didn't understand, and heeding warnings from Reagan that this country's military capabilities were inferior to the Soviet Union's, turned to a candidate who seemed to say he could not only protect what they had but could assure them that their lives would continue to get better. It was in California that Reagan first discovered this constituency.

At the time he was elected Governor of California, the state had long had a land-of-opportunity image of boundless population growth. The image was encouraged by its real estate hucksters and publicists, and augmented by the celluloid exports of Hollywood, which frequently portrayed a glamorous fantasy land that never really existed except on the screen. But by 1967 it was beginning to show a few signs of middle age. Immigration of people from outside the state, a hallmark of California as much as its climate during most of its history, and a torrent during the fifties and early sixties, had started to slow significantly. There was beginning to be less talk about California's benign sun, Hollywood glamour, and boundless opportunities and more talk about its smog, urban congestion, and crime. Its gilt-edged aerospace industry, which had grown with the velocity of a rocket from World War II through the early sixties, was laying off employees and had entered a deep slump. It was a time of social upheaval. The Berkeley campus of the University of California had erupted with the Free Speech Movement in 1964 and the Watts ghetto in Los Angeles blew the following year. College campuses were aflame with dissent over the Vietnam War and other causes, angering many middle class Californians who, like Ronald Reagan, had fought hard to survive the Depression and couldn't understand why the rebellious students didn't appreciate their affluence and their chance for a college education.

California was still a kind of national melting pot where people from elsewhere fled to escape their problems at home and experiment with new lifestyles and new religions, and every so often it still produced a Charles Manson or a Jim Jones. But in other ways it was maturing, becoming more Middle America, less Lotusland. It was becoming more conventional, more conservative, and more apprehensive about challenges to the status quo. The campus unrest; the growing assertiveness of ethnic minorities; the relaxation of many of American society's traditional taboos on behavior involving sex, drugs, and other matters; and other things, including the growing tax burden to finance the social programs of Lyndon Johnson's Great Society, were beginning to cause concern among many people. It was a time of growing public skepticism toward established institutions. It was a skepticism that, ironically, Ronald Reagan shared with the rebellious students who occupied Sproul Hall at Berkeley and taunted him and other leaders in the state. As Jimmy Carter would do a decade later in Washington, Reagan came to Sacramento as an outsider to do battle with the politicians who ruled the state. His target was government, which he said had become too big, too costly, and too inefficient.

If the political pros expected Ronald Reagan, the actor who called himself a "citizen politician" and talked of building a "Creative Society," to execute a political pratfall when he got to Sacramento, they weren't disappointed. By almost all accounts, the first two years of his administration were a dismal failure. But, as he gained experience, most officials who worked with him say that Reagan evolved into an effective, pragmatic Governor who demonstrated great skill in selecting administrators to run state departments, left them alone to do their jobs, and, applying his old skills as an after-dinner speaker, proved highly potent in dealing with recalcitrant legislators by going over their heads to appeal his case to the public via television.

In general, Reagan is given high marks for his performance as Governor. Nevertheless, an analysis of his eight years in Sacramento suggests that if his tenure is measured against what he set out to do, it was less than a success. He arrived in Sacramento with virtually one goal — to cut the size and cost of government. And, while he made headway in many areas, he nevertheless left a state government in 1974 that was considerably larger and taking in far more tax dollars than it had been when he arrived. Yet many of those same officials who praised Reagan's effectiveness as Governor called his claims of savings overblown. An improved economy, which led to the creation of more jobs, and other factors, they said, including the effects of more than 250,000 abortions that were performed on welfare mothers under legislation signed by Reagan in 1967 (he later said he regretted signing the bill) probably did more to cut the welfare case load than Reagan's subsequent welfare eligibility reform.

Despite such quarrels over the details of his accomplishments, the Reagan record in Sacramento is generally regarded as favorable, but his successes followed a rocky road at first. "We weren't just amateurs," his press secretary would say later of the first two or three years in Sacramento, "we were novice amateurs."

Shortly after his inauguration, Reagan announced to Californians that he had made a discovery. The administration of Pat Brown, and by inference the Legislature, had "looted and drained" the state, he said, and had left the Reagan administration with a deficit of almost $200 million. In a speech that had echoes of some of those by his one-time hero, FDR, Reagan declared, "Not since the bleak days of the Depression — during which California was forced to such desperate measures our credit was affected for decades — have we faced such a dark picture . . . California for the last year has been spending $1 million a day more than it has been taking in."

Some of his critics would say then and later that Reagan had overstated the seriousness of the fiscal crisis, but indeed the outgoing Democratic administration had done some tinkering with bookkeeping that had enabled it to avoid asking for an election-year tax increase, and it had left the legacy of a large deficit on Reagan's desk. The new Governor told Californians that the state had no alternative but to raise taxes, and soon the Legislature had passed the largest increase in the state's history, one which brought in almost $1 billion a year in additional revenue. This would be the first of three major tax packages and several smaller ones that raised virtually every category of levy in the state and consistently brought in more money than the Republican administration said they would.

Reagan insisted that he had not forgotten his pledge to "cut, squeeze, and trim," however, and within a few weeks of his inauguration he ordered a freeze on hiring of new state employees and a 10 percent cut in state employment, unveiled a plan to impose tuition at state universities and colleges, and announced a drastic reduction in staffing of state mental hospitals.

But, before long, he had to backtrack on virtually all of his proposed reforms, mostly because he had failed to consult with the legislators whose support he needed for passage of the new laws. He interpreted their reluctance to go along with him, correctly in some cases, to their bowing to pressure from various special interest groups, such as the state employee unions who didn't want to see the size of the state payroll cut, and he pointed this out to the public. As Reagan continued to let the legislators feel his disdain for them, their icy relationship cooled even more. "As far as he was concerned," Bob Moretti, the Speaker of the Assembly and the second most powerful man in Sacramento, recalled, "we were the devil incarnate."

Reagan conceded he had problems. "In the early days of my administration," he would recall, "we had our problems, not only with the members of the other party, but also with the members of our own. In retrospect, we were the new boys in town. There was much to be done and much to be learned — so we learned by doing. . . . I suppose we made all the usual mistakes and tromped, inadvertently, on a lot of toes. Some people described the early days of my administration as a honeymoon. My reply was that if it was a honeymoon, I was sleeping alone. . . . And then, looking around at some of those who allegedly were on the honeymoon with me, I decided that sleeping alone was not such a bad idea. . . ."

By most accounts, it took about two years for Reagan and the staff of mostly political novices he had brought to Sacramento to recognize that to get things done, the executive branch of a government often has to bargain with, cajole, and otherwise court the legislative branch. But it was a full four years before he really came to terms with the Legislature. The turning point probably occurred at a meeting early in 1971 between Reagan and Moretti. Reagan was still not getting many of his reforms through the Legislature, and he was continuing to make his feelings for legislators known to all who would listen.

Moretti, a liberal Democrat who was opposed to virtually every line of the conservative rhetoric Reagan unleashed at any opportunity, telephoned the Governor early in 1971 and said he wanted to see him — alone.

"There was just the two of us," Moretti said later. "We had never been alone. There were always staff people around when we met. I walked into his office and said he had not been impotent. Using his considerable talents to sell a point of view, he had repeatedly taken his case directly to voters via television." The rhetoric had had an effect; public opinion polls perennially gave him high ratings, and it seemed clear that much of the public shared his view of the professional politicians in the Legislature, creating a situation that, in effect, helped persuade Moretti to sue for peace. "Reagan's very good at going to the people," says A. Alan Post, who served as legislative analyst for the state during the Reagan years and was often his critic. "He's extraordinarily good at formulating a political issue to the public and getting them on his side."

Reagan accepted Moretti's offer of a truce and a chance to get one of his most imporant goals — the welfare reform legislation — moving in the legislature. After seventeen days and late nights of negotiations, the Reagan conservatives and the Moretti liberals worked out a classic political compromise. Reagan got reforms significantly narrowing the eligibility for welfare while the liberals got his acceptance of higher benefits and automatic cost-of-living increases for those who remained on welfare. After that, there were more disputes with the Legislature, but he had learned to compromise, and more and more of his proposals passed the Legislature.

"The first two years were miserable," William Bagley, one prominent legislator at the time, remembered, "but either by design or experience or luck, it changed. After the first two years, I think he mellowed and became more pragmatic. I call him a closet moderate." "The way he acted as Governor," Bob Moretti said in later years, "didn't resemble his rhetoric."

Many California politicians and some of his other adversaries, including the officials of the University of California with whom he waged a long and bitter (and ultimately only partially success-ful) battle to reduce its budget, would disagree with this character-ization. But many people who dealt with Reagan later said that as he gained experience, he became less doctrinaire than his public image conveyed.

Wilson Riles, California's highest ranking black official, who in 1970 had defeated Max Rafferty, a strident conservative from the Republican Party's far right wing, to become State Superin-tendent of Public Instruction, said that when he took office he ex-pected problems from a Governor who seemed to sport some of the same political stripes as Rafferty.

Shortly after his election, he recalled, "I called Ronald Rea-gan and asked for an appointment, and he invited me in; I told him that I was in a nonpartisan office and did not want it to be politicized. He agreed to that, and I told him I'd like to have ac-cess to him personally if I saw a problem developing; I was afraid his staff would put a barrier between us.

"He said, 'I fully understand what you mean; you'll have ac-cess. When I was in my former business, we used to say that stand-ins and extras created so much hate that the stars couldn't get the scenes done.' "

Several times over the next four years Riles took positions contrary to the Governor's on issues — on questions, for example, of how much money should be spent on certain educational projects, or how aggressive the state should be in seeking Federal educational aid. Riles remembers Reagan as being open-minded enough to hear out his views, and in a few cases, to change his mind, although in the vast majority of instances his final decision reflected his conservative orientation. Wilson Riles's verdict on the new President: "The bottom line on Ronald Reagan is that he is a conservative and articulates a very conservative position, but, at least in the field of education, which I know about, he did not try to manipulate it in a partisan way, he wasn't a racist, he did his homework, and he was well organized. He was an administrator in the sense that he set the policies and directions and chose good people to carry them out."

Besides his effectiveness in applying pressure on legislators by going to the people (a technique he said he learned from FDR) via television, Reagan, after his difficult first years in Sacramento, discovered the value of a provision of California law giving the Governor a "line item" veto power. It enabled him not only to scuttle individual spending proposals, which had been approved by the Legislature, if he didn't like them, but also to reduce spending on individual items. One of the keys to his success in Sacramento, this law gave him a potent power, which he will not have as President, to shape programs and deal with uncooperative legislators. In all, during the eight years in Sacramento, he used his veto 994 times.

Reagan frequently came under criticism in the press for seeming to have a shallow understanding of some issues, a result of misstatements at news conferences; his slip-ups appeared to reflect his style of running California, with his tendency to delegate authority to subordinates and rely on the four-paragraph "mini memos" to gather information he used in making decisions. His aides, however, defended his reliance on the mini memos as an effective management tool. "Some people joked about them," said Caspar Weinberger, who served Reagan as State Director of Finance and was later Secretary of Health, Education, and Welfare under President Nixon, "but they were backed up by more information. The Governor sought out more information when he needed it. The memos were a very effective way to take a large problem and present a kind of distillation of it that focused the discussion. Then the Governor would apply his own judgment to the problem."

Reagan was also attacked by leaders of organized ethnic minorities for neglecting the poor, for attempting to curtail spending on mental hospitals and trying to impose more control from Sac-

ramento over the state's most powerful independent political fiefdom, the University of California, generally regarded as the finest
system of public higher education in the world, but one that had
relatively little monitoring from the outside on its expenditure of
public funds. Nevertheless, despite these criticisms, when Reagan
turned over the state to his Democratic successor, Edmund G.
Brown, Jr., early in 1975, state expenditures in all three of these
categories had gone up sharply compared to the levels of spending
when he came to Sacramento eight years earlier.

Paradoxically, a man who, as an after-dinner speaker, had
achieved a national reputation in many quarters as a radical right-
winger played a role in enacting three very liberal pieces of legislation: one of the nation's most liberal abortion laws, legislation
giving welfare recipients cost-of-living raises, and imposition of a
very progressive withholding system for the state income tax.

Indeed, the withholding scheme, which Reagan strenuously
objected to for more than two years but finally accepted, poured
an embarrassing cascade of money into Sacramento that continued long after he left. As inflation raised more and more Californians into higher brackets, income tax collections rose from $1.1
billion in the 1969-1970 fiscal year to $2.6 billion by 1974-1975.
Reagan pushed through legislation that rebated part of the growing surplus to taxpayers, and later claimed credit for returning
$5.7 billion to the public — a figure his critics say is exaggerated.
Even with these various rebates, however, the money continued to
roll in, and by 1978 the state had a surplus of more than $6 billion.
This surplus, as well as fast-rising property tax levels, led to the
passage in 1978 of California's controversial Proposition 13,
which drastically reduced property tax collections.

Reagan's legacy of a tax structure that helped lead to the
Proposition 13 explosion has a curious irony. Perhaps sooner than
any other major American politician, he had sensed the tide of
conservatism, including an antipathy toward a distant Federal
government, that would affect much of middle class America in
the later 1970s. Seven years before California voters would pass

Proposition 13, he led an effort to place a similar, if less sweeping, property tax limitation law before the state's voters. The measure lost after a bitter campaign in which public employees spent heavily to defeat it. But Reagan had anticipated the rising public anger over taxes that would boil over as Proposition 13.

In a 1968 interview with James Reston of *The New York Times*, he said: "I am convinced that there is a wave sweeping the land that started in 1966. A wave of desire for a change, dissatisfaction on the part of the people over what's been going on, a feeling that many of the programs that were born with such promise have not born fruit." The same year, in a speech to the Economic Club of New York, he said: "At the moment, there appears to be a panic fear afloat in the air, partly due to a feeling of helplessness, a feeling that government is now a separate force beyond their control, that their voices echo unheeded in the vast and multitudinous halls of government. I do not remember a time when so many Americans, regardless of their economic or social standing, have been so suspicious and apprehensive of the aims, the credibility, and the competence of the Federal establishment. There is a question abroad in the land: 'What is happening to us?' "

As a day-to-day manager and decision-maker in Sacramento, Reagan patterned his style largely after the chairman of a corporation who, most days, got to his office shortly before nine in the morning and left a little before six at night. He delegated considerable authority to subordinates and tended to avoid getting involved in the details of problem-solving, hearing out his subordinates' recommendations and then making his decision based on their advice, usually through a mechanism called a "mini memo," a one-page, four-paragraph summary of a problem and his staff's recommendations on how to solve it.

His style occasionally brought criticism. John P. Sears, who managed his presidential campaign in 1976 and was in charge in 1980 until Reagan fired him early in the year, made some observations about his former boss in an article he wrote for *The Washington Post* after his dismissal: "If his advisers are adequate, there is nothing to fear from President Reagan," he wrote. "But he can be guided, and Presidents who are too easily guided run the risk of losing the confidence of the people."

Sears, who had been accused of, in effect, stage-managing Reagan's campaign, much as a director orchestrates a scene in a motion picture, seemed to agree with this theory. As Governor, Sears asserted, Reagan seldom came up with an original idea, and often, like a performer waiting for a writer to feed him his lines and for a director to show him how to say them, he waited for others to advise him what to do. "He is an endorser," he wrote. "Reagan sat with his California Cabinet more as an equal than as its leader. Once consensus was derived or conflict resolved, he emerged as the spokesman, as the performer."

For all the controversy over his style of possibly relying too much on his staff, legislators generally praised the quality of his appointments. "He had some awfully good people around him," recalled one leader in the Assembly, Joe Veneman. "I think he has a certain talent for attracting good people."

"He depends very much on his staff and the kind of people he gets is going to be very important in what kind of administration he has," Bob Moretti said. "Hopefully they learned, but, if they get a bunch of new people in there from all over the country, I'm afraid you could have the same thing all over again."

Reagan's personnel recruiting was done largely by a group of his "millionaire backers," led by Holmes Tuttle, who said, "He asked us to fill thirty-five or forty of the top jobs. We met for ten hours a day, for weeks, and with the help of other people, we looked for the best people we could find and made the recommendations to Ron. He didn't have to accept them, but I'll say this, in all but one or two cases, he did."

Almost all of the people the search committee nominated for jobs were businessmen or employees of business corporations. Most were Republicans, and most were conservative, but the committee also brought a few moderates into government. Reagan at times was attacked for appointing people to jobs in which they regulated industries in which they had financial interests, but no serious scandals ever touched his California administration. In all, more than 200 business people were brought into state government by Reagan, most of them on short-term "task forces" to recommend ways to improve government efficiency.

Tuttle and his associates began scouting for possible recruits for the Reagan presidential administration early in 1980.

Long after he left Sacramento, a debate would continue over the Reagan years in California. His supporters would say that his record speaks for itself; that he had run an administration that was efficient, slowed the growth rate of government, and left the state in solid financial condition. Some of his critics would describe him as a man who is often unable to grasp the nuances of a complex problem and who, after all, is still a performer — the actor turned after-dinner speaker.

In 1978, his predecessor, Pat Brown, wrote: "I would allow that Ronald Reagan is undoubtedly a sincere man. I also believe that he is in reality what he appears to be: a simple man. His ideas, his philosophy, his perceptions, his comprehension of human affairs and society are also neatly confined to a simple framework of thought and action that permits no doubts and acknowledges no sobering complexities. No wonder his manner is that of a man with utter confidence in his own fundamentalist purity and integrity. The efficient missionary dedicated to eradicating evil."

But Brown argued that life was seldom as simple as it was defined to be by Reagan. "Long before the computer took over our everyday affairs, Reagan was being 'programmed' by writers and directors, molded by producers and sold by promotion and publicity men. Small wonder he still finds it easy to absorb and adopt the thinking of the people around him and that he is most comfortable with the healthy, the successful, and the self-assured — a mirror image of Reagan as he sees himself."

IV

On the Supply Side

Leonard Silk

Ronald Reagan's domestic economic policy for the four years ahead remains something of a mystery. This is not because Reagan has managed, or even tried, to keep his economic views secret. On the contrary, his conservative program, however broadly stated, has been central to his drive for the Presidency, and has been thoroughly exposed. The real problem at this point is that Reaganite economics consists of an inchoate set of numbers, goals, and doctrines (some cautiously conservative, some radically conservative) whose ultimate concrete form will depend on tests of strength between factions in his own party, conflicts between his administration and Congress, and Mr. Reagan's resolution of his own inner conflicts.

On the economic front, the Reagan drive to the White House was powered by two quite different types of conservatives. One was a group of conservative "populists" whose main objective (in the spirit of the California Proposition 13 tax revolt) was to slash taxes, eliminate government programs except in the defense area, slash government regulation, and release the energies of private individuals and private business. This group of populists — and the politicians and economists who sought to give their desires coherence and a rationale in economic theory — was dominated by small- and medium-sized business, farmers, homeowners, retirees, white-collar and even many blue-collar workers: "Middle Americans," many of them with scant sympathy for those below them (especially those on welfare) nor much sympathy toward Big Business. Indeed, many in this populist group have regarded Big Business, and its internationally oriented institutions such as the Trilateral Commission or the Council on Foreign Relations, as a kind of conspiracy designed to serve the interests of multinational corporations rather than that of America. (Earlier in the campaign, George Bush resigned from the Council on Foreign Relations to ward off such attacks.)

But, within the Reagan camp, particularly after he had secured his hold on the nomination, were these very representatives of Big Business and Big Finance, and their professional economic counsellors, who constitute the Republican Establishment. The thinking of this group, though not in clear conflict with that of the populists on every issue, was focused primarily on the importance of checking inflation, stimulating corporate investment, preserving the stability of the international monetary system, balancing the budget, restraining monetary growth — and ensuring the stability, rather than rapid growth, of the domestic economy.

Reagan's economic pitch during the last phase of the campaign was a loose and vague amalgam of these two contrasting conservative approaches, packaged to appeal to a majority of the electorate. In putting together such a package, the Republican Party leader was, after all, doing only what is conventional in democratic politics.

As a successful politician, Reagan knows that the great bulk of the electorate want to see inflation reduced, but they want this to be done in a way that will not mean economic stagnation and worsening unemployment. And, as President, his top domestic priority will be to spur the American economy to a faster rate of growth — if possible, without worsening inflation.

He has sought to portray himself as a conservative version of Franklin D. Roosevelt, and his mission will be to liquidate the "Carter Depression" as Roosevelt did the "Hoover Depression." Obviously, the American economy today is not in a depression; indeed, the 1980 recession, which began in January, almost certainly ended in the third quarter. But, to Reagan, that is a technicality; efforts by Reagan's top economic advisers, Alan Greenspan, the former chief economic adviser to President Gerald R. Ford, and Martin Anderson, of the Hoover Institute, to explain to Reagan that the economy was only in a recession — a short-term downswing — did not touch the real purpose behind his use of the term "depression" to describe the state of the economy under President Carter. His purpose was more than political in the narrow sense; it represented his effort to dramatize his own determination to free the United States economy from the restraints and distortions which he believes have produced a chronic condition of "stagflation" — that combination of stagnating production and persistent inflation.

Although Reagan's economic ideas may be vague and uncertain on how to achieve his objectives, he is clearly committed to a traditional American boosterism, a belief that if only free enterprise can be liberated, the country will once again achieve a strong rate of economic growth, with rising standards of living for all.

It was this philosophy that made him a ready convert to the "supply-side economics" of such advisers as Professor Arthur Laffer of the University of Southern California; Jude Wanniski, a former editorial writer for *The Wall Street Journal*; Representative Jack Kemp of upstate New York; and Senator William V. Roth, Jr., of Delaware. Reagan gave his hearty support to the Kemp-Roth bill for cutting personal income taxes by 30 percent through three successive annual cuts of 10 percent; this was advertised as a "supply-side" tax cut for creating greater incentives to produce, and thereby stimulate real economic growth, which would throw off enough tax revenues to more than pay for the huge tax cuts.

At the heart of the Kemp-Roth bill was the so-called "Laffer curve," named for Professor Laffer. The Laffer curve is a bell-shaped curve which purports to show that when tax rates fall to zero, tax revenues fall to zero, and when tax rates rise to 100 percent, tax revenues also fall to zero, while somewhere between these two extremes is a tipping point — the point of maximum revenue — where an increase in tax rates would only reduce revenues. On either side of this point of maximum revenue there are presumably pairs of points, one higher and the other lower, where either the higher tax or the lower one will yield the same revenue. The lower tax rate of the pair will be preferable, however, because it will spur greater economic output (and incidentally reduce the relative share of government activity in the economic system — a political and not just an economic objective of conservatives).

The Laffer curve certainly had a powerful appeal to Ronald Reagan, through its beautiful and simple logic. But is it true? Critics contend that there is no quantitative evidence of the shape of the curve or where the United States is upon it at the present time. For the "Laffer effect" to work, the tax rate to be cut would have to be higher than at the point of maximum revenue. If rates were already below that point, further cuts in tax rates would produce lower tax revenues. And even if existing tax rates were higher than the point of maximum revenue, cutting rates *too much* would still result in a net loss of revenues. This would widen the budget deficit — which was $59 billion in fiscal 1980. A wider budget deficit would further complicate the problems of holding the growth of the money supply to a moderate, noninflationary rate of increase. If monetary policy were eased to accommodate the bigger budget deficit, inflation could well be aggravated; and if monetary policy were held tight despite the widening budget deficit, interest rates would be driven upward, jeopardizing investment and the economy's growth.

Such criticisms of blind faith in the Laffer curve were made not only by economists of the Democratic persuasion and critics such as the economists at the Federal Reserve Bank of Minneapolis, but by the more conventional or "old guard" conservative economists in Reagan's own camp, such as Alan Greenspan;

George P. Shultz, Secretary of the Treasury under President Nixon and chairman of Reagan's thirteen-member economic policy coordination committee; Arthur F. Burns, the former chairman of the Federal Reserve Board; and Professor Milton Friedman, the Nobel laureate who has served as adviser to Republican Presidents and presidential candidates since Barry Goldwater. Dr. Friedman is the great totemic figure in the Reagan economic stable, whom Reagan exhibited most often when he needed to impress doubters. William E. Simon, who served as Secretary of the Treasury in the Ford administration, began the campaign in Reagan's populist camp but later appeared to have switched to the old-guard conservative side.

As the 1980 campaign wore on and as it became more possible that Reagan would win, the old-guard economists, joined by Walter B. Wriston, chairman of Citicorp and a monetarist follower of Professor Friedman's, sought to moderate Reagan's support for Kemp-Roth; they proposed that the 30 percent reduction in personal income taxes be spread out over a five-year period. But Reagan would not be budged from the three-year period to which he had committed himself, with further personal income cuts to follow, by indexing personal income taxes to the rate of inflation. Kemp-Roth would reduce Federal tax revenues by an estimated $189 billion in 1985.

But Kemp-Roth is not the whole of what Reagan wants to do about taxes. Late in the campaign, in response to the pressures of his old-guard advisers, he switched from supporting the so-called 10-5-3 plan for accelerated depreciation of business assets to a less costly proposal (endorsed by the Senate Finance Committee) of Senator Lloyd Bentsen of Texas to liberalize current depreciation allowances by 40 percent. However, Reagan has remained ambiguous on whether he would later switch back to support of 10-5-3 (the number of years for writing off structures, equipment, and motor vehicles, respectively). Reagan's chief tax adviser, Charls E. Walker, a former Deputy Secretary of the Treasury and leading tax lobbyist, insists that Reagan will indeed return to support of

10-5-3 "as soon as possible." Accelerated depreciation by 10-5-3 would cost the Treasury $60 billion by 1985, compared with $20 billion for the Bentsen proposal.

In addition, Reagan wants to eliminate the tax on oil "windfall" profits, which would cost about $18 billion by 1985. He would, according to Walker, also cut the corporate income tax rate to 44 percent from 46 percent at a cost, depending on when it took effect, of $2 billion to $8 billion.

But there is more: Reagan has advocated repeal of gift and estate taxes, which would cost about $7 billion. He wants to cut taxes on interest and dividends — cost unspecified. He has endorsed tuition tax credits and "urban enterprise zones" to give tax cuts to businesses which invest in distressed urban areas — costs again unspecified.

In all, the various tax cuts proposed by Reagan would add up, as best as one can guesstimate the total, to $250 billion to $300 billion a year by 1985. This would eliminate nearly one-third of Federal tax revenues. Can such deep slashes in taxation be carried through without generating more rapid inflation and worsening the budget deficit?

The question is intensified when one turns to Reagan's plans for rapidly increasing defense spending. During the campaign he was harshly critical of President Carter for doing too little about national defense and for reining in the defense buildup bequeathed to him by President Ford.

After making campaign pledges to cut defense spending by $7 billion to $9 billion, however, Carter shifted to a policy of expanding defense expenditures. The last Carter administration projection of defense expenditures called for defense outlays to rise from $130 billion in fiscal year 1980 to $190 billion in 1983; this plan was designed to produce an increase of 4.5 percent per annum in "real" (adjusted for inflation) defense spending.

The Senate Budget Committee has made projections of defense expenditures showing a rise to $159 billion in fiscal 1981, $187 billion in 1982, $212 billion in 1983, $239 billion in 1984, and $270 billion in 1985. Reagan apparently intends to go at least that far and, if the defense planks in the Republican Party platform are to be carried out, would have to go even further.

The Reagan-dominated 1980 party platform calls for a more "survivable" nuclear missile force, early development of the MX missile, accelerated development and deployment of a new manned B-1 bomber (which Reagan excoriated Carter for abandoning), a modernized air defense system, strategic cruise missiles, and other strategic weapons. The Republican platform rejected the military draft of manpower "at this time" and instead called for "correcting the great inequities in pay and benefits of career military personnel."

How much Reagan's defense buildup will cost is unclear, but it appears likely to mean increasing defense expenditures, excluding the effect of inflation, by 7 to 9 percent a year, if it were to be fully realized. If one assumes that inflation is likely to lift the cost of national defense by an average of 10 percent per year, this would mean increasing defense expenditures to a range of $300 billion to $320 billion by 1985 from the fiscal 1981 level of $159 billion, roughly doubling them in four years.

George P. Shultz said in an interview with the author in mid-October that the defense budget would not be immune from scrutiny for the elimination of waste. But Shultz stressed that nothing was so vital, in Reagan's thinking, as the strengthening of United States defense capabilities.

How can this huge defense buildup be encompassed within a budget plan which also includes huge tax cuts amounting to $250 billion to $300 billion by fiscal 1985?

Solving that budgetary riddle was the task which Reagan's conservative economic advisers — the "old guard," led by Shultz and Alan Greenspan — tackled after the Republican National Convention. They sought to prove that Reagan was not being irresponsible in suggesting that he could greatly increase defense expenditures and cut taxes by about one-third — and still balance the budget and slow down inflation during his first term.

The fruits of their labor were released on September 9, 1980, as "Ronald Reagan's Strategy for Economic Growth and Stability in the 1980s," the economic plan issued before the election and a document which, in stressing the importance of providing "predictability" for consumers and business, was not meant to be a mere piece of campaign propaganda.

The basic objective of the Reagan strategy was to replace economic stagnation and deterioration with a strong thrust toward economic growth. "We must move boldly and decisively," the document said, "to control the runaway growth of Federal spending, to remove the tax disincentives that are throttling the economy, and to reform the regulatory web that is smothering it." Declaring that a new strategy was needed for the 1980s, the Reagan plan quoted Paul McCracken, first chairman of the Council of Economic Advisers under President Nixon, as having stated: "For well over a decade, our strategy has been to reach a better economy by a generalized resistance to spending in order to achieve a balanced budget, thereby winning the right to tax reduction. This predictably has left us with swollen Federal outlays, deficits, and an enervated economy. The road to a stronger budget and a stronger economy by immediately taking needed tax action and directly attaching a shorter leash on spending is at least worth trying."

So the Reaganites elected to go for growth. Only a vigorously growing economy, they maintained, could create the new jobs and the new income that would stop inflation, lower interest rates, and permit them to spend "what we must spend on national defense." Their plan specifically rejected what they called "the economics of scarcity."

The plan was described as comprehensive, with five interlocking parts: (1) "Controlling the rate of growth of government spending to a reasonable, prudent level"; (2) "Reducing personal income tax rates and accelerating and simplifying depreciation schedules in an orderly, systematic way in order to remove the increasing disincentives to work, to save, to invest, and to produce"; (3) "A thorough review of regulations that affect the economy, and prompt action to change those to encourage economic

Early Reagan Platform: A Reagan family portrait (circa 1913) taken in Tampico, Illinois, shows John E. and Nelle Wilson Reagan with their sons, Neil (left) and Ronald. Ronald Wilson Reagan was born in Tampico on February 6, 1911. Although John Reagan suffered from alcoholism and the family had hard times during the Depression, Ronald describes most of his childhood as "one of those rare Huck Finn-Tom Sawyer idylls." *(Wide World)*

"Just One for the Gipper": Ron Reagan on location, dressed for one of his better-known film roles, the dying football star George Gipp in *Knute Rockne, All-American. (Wide World)*

"Twentieth Century Adonis": Reagan was so dubbed in 1940 by the Division of Fine Arts of the University of Southern California, when he was selected as having the most nearly perfect male figure. Here he poses for Professor Merrel Gage's sculpture class. *(UPI)*

Finest Role: In 1942, Ronald Reagan starred in *King's Row* with Ann Sheridan, turning in in of the best performances of his acting career. *(AP)*

Family Man—Take One: Reagan with first wife, Jane Wyman, and their daughter, Maureen. At this point Wyman's movie career was picking up momentum, while Reagan's was tabled during his service in the Army Air Force. Her continued success and his relative lack of it was one of the factors leading to their divorce in 1948. *(Wide World)*

Leading Man: Newlyweds Ronald Reagan and Nancy Davis enjoy a night on the town at the Stork Club in New York City. *(Wide World)*

Politics and Show Business: In Washington, D.C., Reagan, then president of the Screen Actors Guild, holds a small conference before a session of the House Committee on Un-American Activities. *From left:* fellow-actors George Murphy and Robert Montgomery; Robert E. Stripling, chief counsel for the HUAC; and Reagan. *(UPI)*

Henry Salvatori, 79, a Reagan backer since 1966, was one of the early experts in seismic explorations for oil and gas. His company, Western Geophysical, was one of the largest in the industry when it merged with Litton Industries in 1969. Salvatori backed former Governor John Connally of Texas in the presidential primaries, and his relationship with Reagan cooled. Salvatori returned to the Reagan fold when Connally retired from the race.

Theodore E. Cummings, 72 immigrated to the United States from Austria in 1920 and, starting from scratch, proceeded to build a fortune of more than $50 million in the chain-supermarket business. A strong backer of Republican candidates for over twenty years, Cummings met Reagan before his 1966 California gubernatorial campaign and has supported his political efforts ever since. *(The New York Times)*

Justin W. Dart, 73, an outspoken Republican, has known Reagan since 1945, when Reagan was a Democrat. Dart is chairman of the board of Dart and Kraft, a huge California consumer-products company. Dart Industries had one of the largest corporate political-action committees in the United States. *(The New York Times)*

Jack Wrather, 62, is one of the youngest of Reagan's longtime friends and backers. He met Reagan through his wife, Bonita Granville, a former child star who worked with Reagan in one of her films. His company, The Wrather Corporation, is a multimillion-dollar combination of oil, entertainment, and real estate. Wrather is, perhaps the most daring entrepreneur of the group. When asked what role he would play as a Reagan administration adviser, he replied, "I'll be a good friend; I've always tried to be." *(The New York Times)*

Earle M. Jorgensen, 82, is the active chairman of the steel company he founded at the age of twenty-three—one of the few major American steel companies prospering today. A close personal friend of Reagan's, he is a pragmatic businessman whose motto is "Hustle!—that's all." *(The New York Times)*

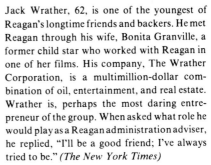

Holmes P. Tuttle, 75, began his career as an automobile salesman in Los Angeles and first met Reagan in 1946 when he sold him a car. A highly successful and well-regarded pillar of the California financial community, Tuttle has been an active political supporter of Reagan since 1964. Tuttle, along with Dart, is considered to be Reagan's closest confidant from the world of big business. *(The New York Times)*

William French Smith, 62, the other junior member of the group, is a highly successful senior partner with one of the two largest law firms in Los Angeles. Smith has known Reagan since before his 1966 campaign for Governor and is his personal attorney. The director of six California companies, Smith is one of the three trustees of Reagan's business interests and is as strongly grounded in business as he is in law. *(Wide World)*

INTO CALIFORNIA POLITICS

Opposite page, top
Party Unity: As Republican gubernatorial candidate, Reagan, then-Senator George Murphy, and former Vice-President Richard Nixon engage in a three-way handshake before walking to the platform of a 1966 California Republican Party victory dinner. *(UPI)*

Opposite page, bottom
The Winner! Reagan greets supporters as he acknowledges his victory as Governor of California over two-term incumbent Edmund G. (Pat) Brown. *(Wide World)*

California Governor: Reagan leads the way as grand marshal of a Veteran's Day parade in Oregon. *(AP)*

Family Man—Take Two: Reagan's second marriage, to actress Nancy Davis, continues successfully after twenty-nine years. Here, during the 1967 Christmas holidays, Governor and Mrs. Reagan, with their two children, Ronald, Jr., nine, and Patti, fifteen, are the picture of the standard American nuclear family. Strong family life ranks high on Reagan's list of publicly propounded values. *(UPI)*

Kerr and Reagan: Governor Reagan talks with Clark Kerr, president of the University of California, before a Board of Regents meeting. Kerr was dismissed as president the next day because he opposed Reagan's proposal to charge tuition in California's public university system. *(UPI)*

Party Man: Governor Reagan makes phone calls on behalf of the Nixon-Agnew ticket in 1972. *(AP)*

Show Biz and Politics—from the Other Side of the Fence: Singer-actor Frank Sinatra, with former Governor Reagan and Mrs. Reagan, at a $500-a-plate dinner to raise campaign funds for the Reagan-for-President Committee in September 1979. *(Wide World)*

All Together Now: At a June 1980 reception for Republican unity, Nancy and Ronald Reagan pose with *(left to right)* George Bush, Phillip Crane, Howard Baker, and John Connally. *(AP)*

Mending Fences: Making his peace with a former rival, GOP presidential-hopeful Reagan speaks with former President Gerald Ford at Ford's home in Palm Springs in June 1980. Ford agreed to support Reagan in his bid to oust President Jimmy Carter. *(Wide World)*

Mapping It Out: Reagan surrounded by top economic advisers *(from left)* George P. Shultz, former Secretary of the Treasury; William Simon, another former Treasury Secretary and bestselling conservative author; Alan Greenspan, former chief economic adviser to President Gerald Ford; Caspar W. Weinberger, former Director of the Office of Management and Budget, and Reagan's expert on control of government spending; and James T. Lynn, former Secretary of Housing and Urban Development and former Director of the Office of Management and Budget. *(Teresa Zabala/The New York Times)*

Waiting It Out: Reagan and members of his family watch the Republican Convention proceedings in their hotel suite in Detroit on July 17, 1980, as the GOP delegates cast their ballots selecting him to be their candidate for President. *(From left):* Son Mike and his wife Colleen, Reagan, son Ron, Jr., wife Nancy, and daughter Patti. *(Wide World)*

Flying High: Nancy Reagan enjoys a light moment during the floor demonstration for her husband's nomination. *(Sara Krulwich/The New York Times)*

A New Beginning: Before a banner proclaiming the GOP Convention motto, delegates rise to attention. *(UPI)*

Acceptance speech at GOP Convention. *(UPI)*

growth"; (4) "The establishment of a stable and sound monetary policy"; and (5) "The restoration of confidence by following a consistent national economic policy that does not change from month to month."

But the details of the strategic plan do not back up this strong, adjectival rhetoric. The control of the growth of Federal spending to "reasonable, prudent" levels would depend on the elimination of many billions of dollars in unspecified waste and fraud. "The reports of waste, extravagance, abuse, and outright fraud," according to the Reagan plan, "are legendary." This waste, it asserted, lies buried "deep in hundreds of Federal programs" and it will take a sustained effort lasting years to extract it.

After the signal failure of Jimmy Carter's elaborate experiment with "zero-base budgeting" to produce significant savings — and the more than doubling of expenditures in California under Reagan's Governorship, with annual state expenditures climbing from $4.6 billion to $10.2 billion despite his promise to "cut and squeeze and trim" — there is widespread skepticism that Reagan can reduce Federal spending by scores of billions of dollars by eliminating waste, fat, and fraud.

Reagan has stressed that he does not mean to hold down Federal spending by eliminating programs. In the televised debate with President Carter on October 28, Reagan, when asked where he would cut government spending if he were to increase defense spending and also cut taxes, said, "Well, most people when they think about cutting government spending, they think in terms of eliminating necessary programs or wiping out something, some service that government is supposed to perform. I believe that there is enough extravagance and fat in government. As a matter of fact, one of the Secretaries of H.E.W. under Mr. Carter testified that he thought there was $7 billion worth of fraud and waste in welfare, and in the medical programs associated with it. We've had the General Accounting Office estimate that there are probably tens of billions of dollars lost in fraud alone, and they have added that waste adds even more to that."

Reagan said he had a program for gradually reducing government "based on these theories." In fact, his strategic plan of September 9 offers two plans for trimming waste and fraud: The first, aiming at "partial achievement," calls for reductions of Federal spending by 2 percent in 1981, 4 percent in 1982, 5 percent in 1983, 6 percent in 1984, and 7 percent in 1985. The second, aiming at "full achievement," would reduce planned Federal spending by 3 percent in 1981, 6 percent in 1982, 8 percent in 1983, and 10 percent in both 1984 and 1985. Taking as its base the projections of the Senate Budget Committee contained in the Second Concurrent Resolution of August 27, 1980, the Reagan plan assumes that, if there were no expenditure cuts, Federal spending would increase from $633 billion in 1981 to $920 billion in 1985. The planned Reagan cuts of "waste and fraud" are projected to total $64.4 billion by 1985, an enormous sum to come out of "fat." That slash in expenditures would be realized indeed if the Reagan spending economies are only partially achieved. The spending cuts would total $92 billion if the Reagan plan to cut spending 10 percent by 1984 were to be fully achieved.

It would be the budgetary coup of the century if cuts of such magnitude could be made by eliminating "waste and fraud," without dropping programs of substance. During the presidential debate, Reagan said he had a task force "working on where those cuts could be made." Indeed, Reagan's strategic plan of September 9 disclosed that "over the next two months, a special Spending Control Task Force, chaired by Caspar Weinberger, former Director of the Office of Management and Budget, will carefully examine all facets of spending control, and then submit a detailed report during the transition on specific ways to search out and eliminate waste and extravagance."

Some of the ideas for cutting waste which are being considered by that Reagan task force are, as *The Wall Street Journal* has noted, "political hot potatoes": lowering cost-of-living increases in Social Security benefits, repealing the minimum wage, allowing states to abolish their food-stamp programs, cutting off Federal housing aid to cities with rent controls, and weakening Federal rules requiring more highway construction work for minority and women subcontractors.[1]

There were other equally controversial proposals submitted to the task force: raising the ages at which Social Security benefits would be payable, revising the consumer price index to produce lower inflation figures, cutting welfare payments by using FBI "strike forces" to look for welfare fraud and by giving states a cash bounty for convicting welfare cheaters, giving states freedom to design and run their own welfare systems, and reducing or eliminating Federal safety requirements on automakers. None of these proposals has yet been accepted by Reagan.

He has, however, announced that he will call for an immediate freeze on the level of Federal employment. But President Carter already had such a freeze in effect months earlier. Caspar Weinberger said the Reagan freeze on Federal hiring would be "more effective" than Carter's had been.

The central logic underlying the Reagan fiscal strategy is the assumption that the tax revenues of the Federal government will, as a result of inflation and real economic growth, increase enormously over the next five years, while expenditures are held well below the growth of revenues. Hence, it is argued, huge tax cuts can still be made consistent with movement toward a balanced budget — and even sizable budget surpluses by 1985.

As a base for their planning, the Republican strategists take the Senate Budget Committee estimates of a rate of real economic growth of 1 to 3.8 percent in the next five years, an inflation rate that declined slowly to 7.5 percent by 1985, and an unemployment rate that comes down to 6.1 percent by that year. On those assumptions, the Senate committee estimated that the revenue of the Federal government would rise to $1,102 billion by fiscal year 1985, an increase of $584 billion over the fiscal 1980 level. Then, if Federal outlays were held to an increase of $920 billion by 1985, the budget would show a surplus of $182 billion in that year. But is this likely to happen? Expenditures may not be held down; the

---

[1] *The Wall Street Journal,* Oct. 24, 1980, p. 1.

states may be unable to pick up Federal programs because they cannot run deficits like the Federal government. And real growth may fall short.

The Reagan plan is designed to overcome what the Democratic economist Walter W. Heller, back in the Kennedy administration, called "fiscal drag," resulting from too heavy a tax burden. For, as the Reagan plan puts it, "this growing tax burden will add even more disincentives to earning, saving, and investing."

The major difference from the Kennedy-Johnson tax cut of 1964, according to Reagan's economists, is that the Democratic tax cut represents "Keynesian" or "demand-side" economics, whereas their own proposed tax cuts are labeled "supply-side." The Republican document states: "Ronald Reagan's tax program is designed to remove disincentives, to stimulate the kind of economic growth that will result in a steady increase in the real take-home pay of the American worker and the removal of uncertainty about job security." Yet the primary effect would be to increase consumption, although there might be secondary effects on investment and the growth of productivity.

After the three-year Kemp-Roth tax cuts of 30 percent are completed in 1983, the Reagan plan calls for indexing for inflation of the personal income tax brackets to prevent inflation from moving taxpayers into higher and higher tax brackets. However, inflation is not to be eliminated but only indexed against.

The Reagan plan also calls for "accelerated depreciation for business to stimulate job-creating investments." For the sake of long-run budget planning, the Reagan document assumes that the Bentsen accelerated depreciation plan, which would reduce business taxes by $20 billion, will be adopted, rather than the 10-5-3 plan, which would cost $60 billion. But this may not stand — if Charles Walker and the big business champions of 10-5-3 prevail.

After allowing for these various proposals for cutting taxes and restraining the growth of Federal spending, within a context of continuing inflation and real economic growth, the Reagan plan projects a decline in the Federal deficit from $59 billion in fiscal 1980 to $27 billion in 1981 and $6 billion in 1982; and it foresees budget surpluses of $23 billion in 1983, $62 billion in 1984, and $121 billion in 1985,[2] *provided that the Reagan administration fully achieves its spending-reduction goal of 10 percent.* If it achieves only its *partial* goal for spending reduction of 7 percent, however, it still projects budget deficits of only $27 billion and $21 billion in 1981 and 1982 respectively, a balanced budget in 1983, and surpluses of $28 billion and $93 billion in 1984 and 1985, respectively.

Will the Reagan domestic economic policy of steep tax cuts and expenditure holddowns work to revive the United States economy while reducing inflation?

The assumptions on which Reagan's plan is based are so uncertain that any economic analysis of his proposed strategy must be regarded as little better than an educated guess. However, the consensus view of forty-two leading economic forecasters, including those of some of the nation's largest businesses, banks, and econometric forecasting services, is that Reagan's proposed tax cuts are excessive and would be likely to "further fuel inflation," as Eggert Economic Enterprises, Inc., summarized the consensus resulting from its survey.

The economists surveyed by Eggert also criticized the vagueness of Reagan's plans for cutting government spending by 7 percent to 10 percent by eliminating "waste and fraud." They were skeptical that he would come close to balancing his budget if he stuck to his plans for greatly increasing defense spending while steeply cutting taxes.

Analysis of the Reagan plan of September 9 by Chase Econometrics, the forecasting subsidiary of the Chase Manhattan Bank, found that the plan, if realized, would make unemployment "significantly higher" and would have "little or no impact on productivity, investment or real economic growth." However, Chase Econometrics found that the Reagan program would have some

---

[2] See Table 1 below.

Table 1
Reagan Budget Projections
FY 1981 to FY 1985
(annual amounts in billions of dollars)

Senate Budget Committee Estimates: Second Concurrent Resolution—August 27, 1980	Fiscal Year				
	1981	1982	1983	1984	1985
Gross National Product	2793	3152	3555	3983	4446
Federal Tax Receipts ("Current Law")	610	712	828	951	1102
Federal Spending	633	710	778	845	920
Defense spending	159	187	212	239	270
Nondefense spending	474	523	566	606	650

Proposed Policy Changes

		1981	1982	1983	1984	1985
(a)	control growth of federal spending	+13	+28	+39	+51	+64
(b)	across-the-board reduction of personal income tax rates and subsequent indexing	−18	−48	−89	−130	−172
(c)	accelerated depreciation to stimulate investment	−4	−13	−18	−19	−20
(d)	additional economic growth	+5	+10	+18	+20	+39
	estimated (deficit) or surplus	(27)	(21)	—	28	93
	as percent of total spending	(4.3%)	(3.0%)	*	3.3%	10.1%
(e)	full achievement of spending reduction goals: additional savings	+6	+15	+23	+34	+28
	estimated (deficit) or surplus	(21)	(6)	23	62	121
	as percent of total spending	(3.3%)	*	3.0%	7.3%	13.2%

* Less than one percent
Source: Reagan/Bush Committee, Sept. 9, 1980

effect in bringing down the rate of inflation, primarily through its cuts in government spending — assuming, of course, that the advertised cuts of $64 billion to $92 billion were to be realized in the next four years.

The Chase analysis found that, if the Reagan plan were to be implemented, real gross national product — the economy's total output of goods and services, adjusted for inflation — would rise by only one-tenth of 1 percent in 1981, and by about 3 percent annually thereafter through 1985.[3] Inflation would be 9 percent in 1981 and would come down gradually to 7.1 percent in 1985. But unemployment would reach 8.9 percent in 1981 and hang on at a 9 percent rate, reaching 9.2 percent in 1985. This implies that the number of jobless workers would increase from 9.5 million in 1981 to 10.5 million in 1985, as the work force continued to grow.

Econometrics being the uncertain science it is — and the Reagan plan being as vague as it is — no one should take the Chase analysis or any other too literally. And if one changed the assumptions in the Reagan plan — for instance, by assuming that while President Reagan might get most of the tax cuts he sought, he would achieve hardly any of the multibillion-dollar expenditure reductions he is proposing — the outlook would be for greater inflation and less unemployment.

However, Reagan's supply-side economists and politicians contend that conventional economic analysis underestimates the impact of his economic strategy and free-enterprise philosophy on individual and business incentives, efforts, and confidence. They say it will make an enormous difference to real growth to get government off the back of the private economy. The Reagan plan calls for "a thorough and systematic review of the thousands of Federal regulations that affect the economy," contending that in

---

[3] The Reagan estimates, as set forth in the strategic plan for growth and stability of September 9, 1980, themselves project that the program of tax cuts, growing to a total of $192 billion by fiscal year 1985, would add only $39 billion to nominal GNP in that year. The additional economic growth resulting from the fiscal stimulus in the preceding years is estimated by the Reagan advisers as $5 billion in 1981, $10 billion in 1982, $18 billion in 1983, and $20 billion in 1984. See Table 1 above.

many cases "regulations have gone to extremes and become counterproductive."

President Reagan intends to propose a requirement that any proposed regulation be accompanied by an "economic impact statement" so that purported benefits can be weighed against the effect of the regulation on jobs and the economy. He wants to work with Congress to tighten the provision of any new legislation to limit the scope of bureaucrats in formulating and interpreting regulations. And he says that, along with spending control, the appointees in a Reagan administration will have, as one of their highest priorities, the task of "analyzing every Federal regulation under their jurisdiction, to see if these regulations are needed."

Reagan has had little to say about monetary policy. He is calling for a "sound, stable and predictable monetary policy," and says that the Federal Reserve Board is, and should remain, independent of the Executive branch. But he notes that the President nominates those who serve on the Federal Reserve Board (which usually has plenty of turnover, especially when administrations change) and that his appointees will be "men and women who share his commitment to restoring the value of the American dollar, and who believe in a sound, stable, and predictable monetary policy."

Such views are consistent with the doctrines of his most famous economic adviser, Professor Friedman. But such monetary policies, stressing strict control of the growth of the money supply, could lead, within the context of steep tax cuts and unbalanced budgets, to chronically high interest rates, which would tend to hurt financial markets and arrest investment and the rate of economic growth.

Reagan and his advisers argue that public and business confidence in his conservative approach to economic policy will overcome the obstacles to growth. They contend that *steadiness* — in contrast to the frequent changes in policy by President Carter — will ensure stronger growth. "There is probably nothing," they say, "that undermines economic growth more than widespread uncertainty about the future actions of government. In a Reagan administration, every effort will be made to establish and begin to implement economic policy early — within the first ninety days — and then to stick to the essentials of this policy."

One of the first actions President Reagan is likely to take on assuming office will be to send a tax package to Congress recommending an immediate 10 percent cut in personal income tax rates, the first installment of a 30 percent reduction over three years, as specified in the Kemp-Roth bill. He will surely include in the package other proposals to reduce taxes on business.

It seems probable that Congress, already prepared to cut taxes on its own by some $39 billion in fiscal 1981, would go along with the first-year part of the Reagan plan. But thereafter Reagan is likely to have a much harder row to hoe with Congress on both taxes and spending, not only because Democrats will still be in the majority in the House but also because proposed spending cuts are bound to provoke strong opposition from particular constituencies. Furthermore, excessive tax cutting, leading to worse budget deficits, would probably be resisted by Congress as inflationary.

To be sure, Reagan himself is no inflationist. The strongest single economic plank in the Reagan-dominated Republican Party platform was its denunciation of inflation and its attack on President Carter for aggravating inflation during his four-year term. Reagan could adduce ample justification of modifying the tax and spending components of his program, should these later be found to conflict with the objectives of balancing the budget and checking inflation.

Pragmatism — defined as a willingness to depart from an earlier course, as required by political circumstances — is a well-established Reagan trait. As Governor of California, not only did he more than double state expenditures, as we have noted, but he presided over three major tax increases. These were large enough, however, to yield budget surpluses, and he gave back part of the surpluses through tax reductions and rebates. John Schmitz, a conservative Republican state Senator, said of Reagan's tax and spending performance in California: "He didn't do any flashing here."

His more traditionally conservative advisers, including both the economists who served in the Nixon and Ford administrations and the businessmen who have been behind Reagan for many years, will be eager for him not to be fiscally irresponsible. Yet he still seems determined to take some risks for faster growth. He appears likely, therefore, to try to build an administration in which supply-siders and traditional conservatives can live and work together. Speaking of past struggles between the two groups, Alan Greenspan says, "It's a fight within a family — not one between the Hatfields and the McCoys." But the old-guard conservatives — such as Greenspan himself — appear to have emerged as the dominant group around the new President.

Reagan has the reputation among those who have watched him closely, not only during his two terms as Governor but during the recent presidential campaign, as a man who handles his principles flexibly, as required to meet changing political or economic objectives. "You want a principled man, which Reagan is," says Professor Milton Friedman. "But he is not a rigidly principled man, which you don't want," he adds. Some Reagan observers — advisers as well as foes — put the same point more negatively, saying they doubt that he has any deep, long-run convictions, but has the political sense not to shift positions too much or too often in the short run.

The obstacles to a successful Reagan effort to implement his strategic plan — to slash taxes, hold down government spending, and deregulate business, thereby achieving, as his slogan goes, "full employment without inflation through economic growth" — lie in both Congress and within his own party. But the most important obstacle doubtless is the conflict among his objectives and the constraints imposed by the structure of the budget and the high cost of defense and other ongoing government programs, such as Social Security, which Reagan does not intend to cut.

The greatest question about a Reagan administration is

whether it would cure or worsen inflation. Earlier Reagan entertained the idea of trying to solve the inflation problem by returning to the gold standard, but such advisers as George Shultz, Alan Greenspan, and Milton Friedman appear to have convinced him that the idea is far too risky. Inflation at a fairly high rate, at least, appears to lie ahead. Indeed, Reagan's fiscal plan depends on accepting a fairly high rate of inflation — in the 8 to 10 percent range — to achieve the tax cuts and budget balance he seeks. He is bound to have great difficulty in getting the "comprehensive" program he wants through Congress and through the resistances of various interest groups in the four years ahead.

Post-election realism will probably force President Reagan and his close aides to adjust their program — which has served its essential purpose of selling the Republican Party's candidate to the nation — to less risky proportions. If the program is not trimmed, especially in the huge tax cuts it has advertised, the nation may be in for an exciting adventure in economic policy-making — with a markedly diminished role for the Federal government, and a seriously worsened budgetary and inflationary problem.

V

Free Trader

Leonard Silk

Ronald Reagan's overall approach to international economic policy is an extension of his domestic economic philosophy. That is: an aversion to government interference with free private enterprise and free markets. Thus, he favors free trade as a way to provide greater opportunities for American business abroad, benefits for consumers at home, and a check to inflation.

But Reagan is also a practical politician who is likely to be responsive to pressure groups making a strong and insistent case that they are being injured by free trade and foreign competition. The likelihood is that, in a crunch, Reagan's political pragmatism would win out over his free-trade ideology. He has already hedged his position carefully. When asked whether he would impose limits on the importation of such goods as automobiles and steel that are blamed for causing unemployment in the United States, he said: "I would not want to resort to protectionism. That kind of protectionism leads to retaliation. But I think the President could tell other countries, 'Look, we believe in free trade; but we also believe in fair trade. Now, you've got to play the game fairly as we do.' " By such statements Reagan has left himself room to impose quotas or other trade barriers on countries like Japan, against whom a case can be made that they have "unfairly" excluded American goods.

Reagan has firmly indicated that protectionism would not be the major thrust of his policy. "My main belief," he insists, "is that we will become more competitive in the world by removing from the backs of industry in America unnecessary Federal regulations." He offers data to support this position, saying that the steel industry is covered "by 5,600 regulations administered by twenty-seven separate government agencies." Many of these regulations, he says, are conflicting, "so business is left having to say, 'How can we follow this regulation without violating one from another?' "

While touring an almost deserted steel mill, the Jones and Laughlin Corporation's Campbell Works in Youngstown, Ohio, in early October 1980, Reagan largely stuck to his tradition that over-regulation by government was the cause of the industry's decline. He told workers, "I think it is enough to make someone very angry. It certainly has me." He blamed excessive environmental and other controls for the closing of that and other steel plants and vowed to "get the Government off the backs" of the steel industry. As President, he intends, he says, to fight for less stringent regulation of both steel and coal, and presumably other industries as well. "People are ecology, too," he said. But on other occasions, as in smog-ridden Los Angeles, he softened his anti-environmental stand.

Similarly, on foreign economic policy, Reagan is no hobgoblin of consistency. In the presence of anxious steel workers, he blamed the steel industry's woes not only on "excessive government regulations and punitive taxing policies" but also on "cheap imported steel" for forcing "tens of thousands" of layoffs. The free-trade economists in his camp dismiss such bows in the direction of protectionism as momentary lapses.

On the whole, he has held to a free-trade doctrine with reasonable consistency. In the face of mounting pressures from the auto industry and the United Auto Workers to restrict imports of foreign — especially Japanese — cars and trucks, Reagan during the campaign reiterated his opposition to quotas on imports, declaring, "By inducing retaliation by our trade partners, quotas could deprive American workers of valuable foreign markets and reduce, rather than increase, demand for American-made cars."

He did not, however, reject the idea of some help to the American auto industry. He proposed a moratorium on future regulations and a review of existing regulations on autos, new tax breaks to encourage retooling for the production of small cars, and repeal of Federal gasoline allocation rules which, he contended, have in the past led to gasoline lines and a drop in the demand for U.S. autos.

The growth of international trade since World War II, says Reagan, has helped to improve the living standards of all the trading partners. "One of the best ways to promote economic growth in the future," he adds, "is to continue to expand our trade with other nations." He emphasizes that American exports provide one-sixth of all private-sector jobs in the United States. He means to safeguard or expand the number of those jobs, not by excluding imports, but by increasing American access to foreign markets. He inveighs against countries that "impose barriers to our exports and unfairly subsidize their own industries," and has promised to work to prevent such unfair trade practices from penalizing American producers. But he believes it "far better serves our own interests, and those of the world, to aggressively pursue a reduction in foreign nations' trade barriers rather than to erect more barriers of our own."

Reagan has committed himself to a policy of vigorous export promotion. As President, he means to press foreign leaders to open their countries up more freely to American goods. "In my meetings with other heads of state," he has said, "I would be a strong advocate for the sale of our commodities in foreign countries, giving those trade questions the kind of direct personal presidential thrust they deserve." Reagan urges commodity producers across the United States to learn from "the excellent example of

Iowa's corn and soybean growers and establish a check-off system" to support market development overseas, calling such programs "a tribute to our free economy" which would have his strong endorsement and cooperation. And he warns that he would "not stand idly by while foreign governments heavily subsidize their farmers for the purpose of undercutting our products in the marketplace."

Reagan's generally liberal approach to foreign trade will face serious obstacles both at home and abroad. At home, such major industries as autos and steel, fearful of their survival at anything like their present size, are demanding greater protection and stressing their importance to national security and to the future of the United States as an industrial power.

Some auto industry leaders have in private been expressing their fears that they cannot compete effectively with the Japanese auto producers because their employees work together so enthusiastically and effectively, while being paid at only about 40 percent of the wage rate collected by American workers. The American auto producers also maintain that, with every other industrial nation imposing greater restrictions against Japanese products, the United States takes more Japanese imports than it can sustain, unless the American auto industry is to atrophy or at least be greatly reduced in size. U.S. auto producers, who are likely to have strong influence within the Reagan administration, are likely to press hard for protection in some form, whether mandatory or through "voluntary" self-restraint by the Japanese. Similar pressures will hit the Reagan administration from steel, electronics, and other industries feeling the effects of unemployment, sluggish growth, and worldwide excess capacity.

Foreign governments, feeling the same sort of protectionist pressures from their own industries and labor unions, are likely to resist changing their trade policies in a more liberal direction, just to remove the Reagan charge of "unfairness." Actions to retaliate against foreign discrimination could indeed, as Reagan realizes, backfire on the United States. The threat of growing protectionism has worsened throughout the world under the impact of recession, inflation, and balance-of-payments weakness, all of which have been intensified by the chronic squeeze on oil supplies and prices by the Organization of Petroleum Exporting Countries. Holding the fort against such powerful impulses toward protectionism will be one of the great tasks facing President Reagan.

If the Reagan administration is to hold to liberal trade policies, it will have to pursue domestic policies for spurring economic growth, both at home and internationally. Reagan's support for free trade is therefore closely linked to his proposed "supply-side" tax cuts for increasing incentives and productivity and for raising the level of national savings and investment.

The United States emerged from World War II as the strongest economy in the world by far and the national leader of the non-Communist nations. It assumed the mission of helping its war-damaged allies, as well as it enemies, Japan and Germany, to rebuild their shattered economies. This mission was considered not one of pure altruism but of enlightened self-interest. But what went wrong? Why did the United States lose ground, as other countries strengthened?

One major reason is that stronger investment efforts enabled the industrial countries, especially Japan and West Germany, to achieve greater technological progress than the United States. Since 1960, domestic investment as a percentage of gross national product ran at annual rates of only 16 to 18 percent in the United States compared with 32 to 34 percent in Japan and 22 percent to 27 percent in West Germany. Indeed, the United States for the past two decades has had the lowest domestic investment rate of any major industrial nation.

The Reagan fiscal policy is designed to change that situation, and thereby to restore the productivity and competitiveness of United States industry in the world economy. Hence, confronted by sharp criticism of many traditionally conservative economists of his tax proposals, which they warned would exacerbate inflation, Reagan has not wavered from his support of the Kemp-Roth bill to reduce Federal income taxes by 30 percent during the first three years of his administration. In addition, he means to press

Congress to provide other tax cuts for business, especially faster write-offs of investment in new plant, equipment and motor vehicles.

But Reagan hopes to combine such fiscal stimulus, urged by the "supply-siders" in his camp, such as Representative Jack Kemp of upstate New York, Senator William V. Roth, Jr., of Delaware, and Professor Arthur Laffer of the University of Southern California, with the more cautious fiscal and monetary approach of such Republican economic stalwarts as Alan Greenspan, George P. Shultz, Arthur F. Burns, and — perhaps most influential of all — Professor Milton Friedman, the Nobel laureate. In giving the top policy role to this latter group, the "old guard," however, Reagan has still insisted that fiscal and monetary caution be combined with the stimulus preached by his "supply-siders" or "populists."

Reagan's two sets of economic advisers, the old guard and the populists, differ not only on domestic but on international monetary policy. The populists favor a return to the gold standard, with fixed exchange rates between the dollar (and other currencies) and gold, while the old guard warns that such a return to the gold standard would be extremely hazardous in the present worldwide inflationary environment.

Asked in the spring of 1980 whether he was seriously considering a return to the gold standard, Reagan replied: "Yes, I know it would be complicated to go back to a gold standard as such, but I am looking at a de facto gold standard. Suppose the United States set a date and said we are going to mint a coin based on the value of gold at that time. Once people realized they could take paper dollars and buy a gold coin of the same face value, they probably wouldn't bother to, and it would stabilize the value of the dollar." This Reagan reasoning was apparently picked up from a memo by Professor Laffer. As an ex-actor, Reagan seems inclined to reel off scripts that have been given to him and that he has learned, but frequently appears not to have gone in with understanding beyond the words of the script.

Until late in the 1980 political campaign, Reagan unquestionably still was satisfied to go along with those economic advisers who had been calling for a return to the gold standard. He accepted, though without fully committing himself, their contention that the return to gold would bring stability to the international monetary system and would help stop inflation at home. As George Shultz, a champion of flexible exchange rates — indeed, it was he who negotiated them during the Nixon administration — agrees, Reagan remains seriously interested in the possibility of an eventual return to gold. The conservative economists of the old guard, such as Shultz, who strongly favored flexible exchange rates, apparently succeeded in convincing Reagan that since Americans could buy and sell gold freely, and since gold owners, public or private, were free to turn gold into coins, in effect we were already close to being back on a gold standard. Meanwhile, it would be too risky to try to formalize a fixed-rate exchange system.

Reagan's support for gold found its way into the Republican Party platform, in a clause adopted unanimously by the twenty-five-member subcommittee on fiscal and monetary affairs chaired by Senator Roth. Although the clause did not mention the word "gold," it might well have, since it declared: "The severing of the dollar's link with real commodities in the 1960s and 1970s, in order to pursue economic goals other than dollar stability, has unleashed hyperinflationary forces at home and monetary disorder abroad, without bringing any of the desired economic benefits. One of the most urgent economic tasks in the period ahead will be the restoration of the dependable monetary standard — that is, an end to inflation."

However, in the final phase of the election campaign, Reagan downplayed his commitment to a return to the gold standard. He seemingly accepted the logic of Greenspan, Shultz, and Friedman that it would be too risky to "put the cart before the horse" by trying to impose a gold standard and fixed rates of exchange upon the United States and other nations before world price stability had been achieved. The old guard contended that fixing the dollar at too high a price in terms of gold would make American goods uncompetitive in world markets while setting the dollar's rate too low would result in a massive outflow of United States gold; and possibly, as Greenspan warned, "the loss of all the gold in Fort Knox overnight." The result of such warnings appears to have been a cooling of Reagan's zeal for an early return to gold, but without dissuading him of its ultimate desirability. It now seems highly improbable that Reagan as President would press for going back to the gold standard, as long as his top advisers include such men as Greenspan, Shultz, and Friedman.

Reagan's elevation of old guard economists to the primary role in his administration, together with his choice of George Bush, the moderate Republican (earlier denounced by Reagan supporters as a representative of the "Eastern Liberal Establishment") suggests that Reagan means to be pragmatic and to play "coalition politics" in the White House, while seeking to retain the support of Republican right-wingers, many of whom ardently desire a return to the gold standard.

But he now seems certain to avoid precipitating action on gold that might produce a crisis for the dollar and the world monetary system. He would face grave difficulties in persuading other countries to go along with any plan to rigidly fix exchange rates. As Dr. Otmar Emminger, the former president of the West German Bunderbank, has observed, floating exchange rates — rates that are free to move up and down with the supply and demand for currencies — have permitted the growth in world trade, despite worldwide inflationary disorder and the energy crisis. Floating rates have helped to curb protectionism and have enabled several major countries to eliminate capital controls. These are all goals that Reagan himself favors. In addition, Emminger notes, where attempts have been made to stabilize exchange rates with divergent inflation rates, as in the case of the European Monetary System, inflation has been worsened, with the high rates of price increase in some countries transmitted to countries with lower rates of inflation. The reason is that the flight of money from high-inflation to low-inflation countries tends to expand the money supply in the low-inflation countries and thereby drives up prices.

Opposition nowadays to fixed exchange rates, which is the real meaning and core of a gold standard, is by no means only a conservative view of economists such as Otmar Emminger or Milton Friedman, but is a position just as strongly held by such liberal economists as Professor Paul A. Samuelson, another Nobel Prize winner, Professor James Tobin, and other leading economic advisers to Democratic administrations.

The Reagan administration's foreign economic policy will be closely linked to its foreign policy and national security objectives. Reagan seems more determined than President Carter was to put greater pressure on members of OPEC to moderate their price actions and to invest their surplus earnings in the poor oil-importing countries of the Third World, if they are to expect continued United States economic, technical, and military support. He is also likely to be more aggressive in pressing Europe and Japan for their backing of a more determined United States effort to insure Western access to energy supplies in the Middle East and other OPEC countries.

The United States' allies might regard a more aggressive Reagan foreign and economic policy as excessively nationalistic and potentially dangerous to their own interests. The problem facing President Reagan will be to reconstruct a more forceful United States foreign economic and defense policy that will avoid shocking the Western alliance into still worse disarray.

Both by the evidence of his own public remarks and the judgment of advisers who have worked closely with him, Ronald Reagan lacks depth or detailed knowledge of economic affairs. However, his record as Governor of California suggests that he will be willing to appoint competent officers and give them the scope and authority to get the job done. It is therefore important, in trying to assess the likely economic policies of a Reagan administration, to go beyond Reagan's own statements to those of his key advisers. That task has been facilitated by the publication by the Hoover Institution of a thick volume, "The United States in the 1980s," to which twenty-three experts, many of whom are likely to serve the Reagan administration, contributed.

The principal chapter on foreign economic policy, written by Professor G. M. Meier of Stanford University, stresses that American foreign economic policy must foster trade liberalization, promote guidelines for exchange-rate intervention by national governments, strengthen the role of private international finance, and expand opportunities for the exports of developing countries.

The United States is urged to pursue close policy coordination with Europe, Japan, and the newly industrialized countries, and must operate in the context of a multipolar power structure. Foreign economic policy cannot avoid being shaped by the state of the domestic economy, Professor Meier observes, for unless inflation and unemployment can be lessened, pressures will mount for controls over foreign trade and capital movements. But, conversely, an open and competitive world economy can contribute much to domestic economic expansion. Reagan appears to have taken that lesson to heart.

The disarray of the international economy has already had adverse effects on the United States economy, and the new Reagan administration will have to strive to pursue domestic economic goals of full employment and economic stability without external imbalance. Unfortunately, that goal today seems more distant than it was a decade ago. The temptations are greater — and still more dangerous — to resort to defensive economic nationalism, or an East-West or North-South confrontation.

Professor Meier warns that there is always the danger that the regulation of international economic conduct will be abandoned either to simple unilateral action or to tests of bargaining power between nations. To avoid the dangers of nationalism and policy competition among nations, he urges better policy coordination. "In the last analysis," he concludes, "not American foreign economic policy alone but policy coordination and supranational decision units will be required to reduce the tensions and conflicts. . . . In this wider approach to policymaking, more progress can be made toward international deregulation and the greater employment of full and efficient use of global resources."

Increasing the supply and use of resources, both human and material, will be essential in the years ahead to prevent inflation — without resorting to the periodic spells of economic slump and high unemployment. In an increasingly closely integrated world economy, such policies for growth will have to be international in scope, for a single nation — even one as huge as the United States — that presses for expansion alone might wreck its balance of payments and currency, and thereby worsen its inflation.

But can the United States and its partners learn to work together in a way that is mutually beneficial, or will nation after nation be driven to adopt protectionist policies, ultimately causing the world economy to stagnate and disintegrate, as happened in the 1930s — with devastating consequences for world peace? That is the life-and-death issue that confronts President Reagan and his new administration.

Reagan's commitment to increasing United States defense capabilities is presented by his foreign policy advisers not as a burden to the American economic performance but as a means of strengthening the United States economic role abroad. They contend that, unless the credibility of the United States as a powerful military ally, especially vis-à-vis the Soviet Union, is enhanced, countries in Western Europe and Asia will be progressively less willing to agree to economic and other concessions, to liberalize trade further, or to follow the United States' lead in demanding reliable access to supplies of energy and raw materials. Lacking belief in American political and military power, according to the Reagan camp's view, other countries would be reluctant to share the cost of collective defense and to regulate economic relations with the Communist and developing countries on a common basis with the United States.

There is no question that Reagan gives paramount emphasis to strengthening the United States militarily, and shows no evidence of concern that high and rapidly rising defense expenditures could weaken the American economic performance, by diverting resources from civilian uses, where they might strengthen American productivity, to military uses, which could exacerbate inflationary pressures.

The efforts of a Reagan administration to intensify United States and allied pressures on Communist, oil-producing, and Third World countries could risk worsening U.S. relations not only with those blocs but also with Western Europe and Japan. Unless handled with remarkable skill, the United States' allies might regard a more aggressive Reagan foreign and economic policy as excessively national.

VI

Arms and the Man

Richard Burt

It was only ten o'clock in the morning, but the senior aide in Jimmy Carter's White House slumped down in his chair, tired and depressed. The date was April 25, 1980, and only three hours earlier, the President had made a brief announcement telling the nation that a daring mission to send Army commandos into Teheran to rescue fifty-three American hostages had ended in tragic failure somewhere in the Iranian desert. Many of the details surrounding the fiasco were still unclear, and the public had yet to view the scenes of the charred and twisted wreckage of American helicopters on the T.V. news. Nevertheless, the weary White House official expressed few doubts over what the political impact of the abortive rescue mission would be. "National defense has emerged as a bigger issue in 1980 than any campaign in recent history, with Ronald Reagan and the other Republicans arguing that we have become a second-rate power. The rescue mission is going to convince a lot of folks that Reagan is right."

Seven months later, the White House aide's prediction was borne out at the polls. And as he and his colleagues began updating their job résumés, a new team of national security specialists prepared to enter the government, all dedicated to restoring "a margin of safety" to the country's defenses. At the Pentagon, there was undisguised jubilation among ranking military officers, who had let it be known during the campaign that they were disturbed about the state of American military readiness. On Wall Street, meanwhile, Reagan's victory resulted in a surge in the prices of aircraft and other defense-related stocks.

With hindsight, the election capped off a decade-long shift in public opinion toward defense spending and American military power. In the early 1970s, with the United States engaged in the painful process of disengaging from the Vietnam War, the defense budget declined for the first time since the 1950s. President Gerald Ford's budget projections in 1976 called for large increases in military spending, but the voters chose Jimmy Carter, who had campaigned on the promise of slashing the Pentagon budget by at least $5 billion, a pledge he was never able to carry out. Reagan, on the other hand, campaigned hard on the theme of rebuilding the American military and was the beneficiary of a new national mood that was shaped not by Vietnam, but by the hostage crisis in Iran, the Soviet invasion of Afghanistan, and turbulence in central America.

In contrast to Jimmy Carter, Ronald Reagan is clearly comfortable with military power. A veteran of World War II (he worked with the Culver City Commandos, the first motion picture unit of the Army Air Corps), Reagan believes, like many in his generation, that military strength is a prerequisite for peace. Hitler, the Japanese attack on Pearl Harbor, North Korea's invasion of the south, all of these could have been avoided had the United States and its allies kept their defenses in good order. Thus, there is little of the ambivalence about American military power that grew up during the Vietnam era and seemed to inform Jimmy Carter's view of the world. A nuclear submariner, Carter combined an engineering approach to military problems with an almost religious zeal for limiting the arms race with Moscow through negotiation. Reagan, on the other hand, is said by close friends to trust the judgment of military professionals, believing that many of the nation's most serious strategic mistakes, including Vietnam, stemmed from attempts by civilian "systems analysts" in the Pentagon and at private think tanks to usurp the rightful role of the military. At the same time, he has repeatedly said that the State Department has placed too much trust in arms control talks and that time after time naive American diplomats have been outfoxed by Russians sitting across the negotiating table.

But while Reagan has been given a mandate to strengthen the military, it is not clear how easily or fast he will be able to do this. Reagan's commitments to cut taxes and reduce government spending obviously clash with his goal of spending more for defense. If his economic advisers do find a way to add to the Pentagon budget, Reagan and his national security advisers will still face the equally daunting task of deciding how the extra money should be apportioned: to upgrade strategic nuclear forces, to equip the Army and the Marine Corps to fight a war in the Persian Gulf, or to raise military pay to stem the hemorrhage of technical specialists from all the services?

During the campaign, Reagan and his aides addressed few of these tough questions, preferring instead to concentrate on what he called "the lesson of history, that among the great nations only those with strength to protect their interests survive." But this struck a chord with an electorate that had become worried about Soviet military gains and emerging problems within the American defense establishment.

The Soviet buildup has created a number of novel military challenges for the West. Moscow's drive into Afghanistan and its growing fleet of cargo planes and ships have made military planners deeply concerned about the security of oil supplies from Saudi Arabia and other Persian Gulf nations. The introduction of a new generation of highly accurate intercontinental missiles, particularly the SS-18 "heavy" rocket, has made the U.S. Air Force's 1,000 Minuteman missiles vulnerable, for the first time, to Soviet nuclear "first strike." Moscow's deployment, meanwhile, of new intermediate-range missiles and bombers directed against Western Europe has erased the traditional American advantage in this area. These problems have coincided with a number of worrisome trends within the American defense establishment: the rising cost of recruiting and retaining manpower, a product of introducing the all-volunteer army forces, which has drained funds for new weapons programs; the growing complexity of new weapons, which has led to maintenance problems and lowered readiness; and a shrinking industrial base for military production, which limits what could be produced in a national emergency.

About halfway into his Presidency, Jimmy Carter began to take steps to remedy these problems. Although strongly attached to obtaining a new treaty limiting strategic nuclear arms, he approved an Air Force plan to develop a $33 billion mobile missile, the MX, meant to counter any Soviet "first strike" threat. In the wake of the Soviet drive into Afghanistan, he called for the Pentagon to take existing Army and Marine units and form a 100,000-man "rapid deployment force" for use in future crises in the Middle East. Responding to the Soviet nuclear buildup in Europe, he prodded the North Atlantic Treaty Organization countries to accept a plan for deploying American cruise missiles in West Germany and four other nations.

To the new breed of defense advisers around Reagan, these responses were too little and too late. Typical of the new breed is William R. Van Cleave. A tough-spoken, forty-five-year-old ex-Marine who now teaches at the University of Southern California, Van Cleave not only criticizes the Carter team's defense record, but he is equally skeptical of policies pursued during the Nixon-Ford era, when Secretary of State Henry A. Kissinger sought a détente with Moscow based on arms control accords. A member of the Pentagon task force assigned to the strategic arms talks in the early 1970s, Van Cleave believes that Kissinger mistakenly thought that arms control agreements would freeze Moscow's military buildup. "We have a decade of experience with SALT," Van Cleave said recently. "The objective and aspirations we shared in 1976 have not been borne out. The trends have been adverse — toward increased instability, less viable forces, toward Soviet superiority, rather than parity. They've been toward the need to spend more money on strategic forces and they've been accompanied by more bellicose and aggressive Soviet behavior."

Van Cleave and other defense specialists in the Reagan entourage challenge the Carter defense program on both philosophical and technical grounds. Probably most important, they believe, as Van Cleave said, that Moscow is "embarked upon a determined quest for military superiority." Lacking any devotion to military parity with the United States, Moscow, they assert, can only be dissuaded from continuing its steady military buildup by the threat of an even larger American military response.

The concept that Moscow is determined to achieve superiority has led Reagan and his team to conclude that the United States should not be embarrassed about seeking the same. "Since when has it been wrong for America to be first in military strength?," Reagan asked in a speech to the American Legion in August. "How is military superiority dangerous?" In addition to rejecting the concept of military parity with Moscow, a Reagan defense policy also envisages a worldwide role for American armed forces. For example, a confidential paper prepared for Richard V. Allen, Reagan's top national security adviser, during the campaign says that "while the United States does not assume global responsibility for international peace and stability, no area of the world is beyond the scope of American interest if control or influence by a hostile power threatens American security."

The policy paper, entitled "Strategic Guidance," contains other principles for shaping American defense policy that represent important departures from current concepts:

¶ The United States should explore the possibility of defending against a nuclear attack by heavily investing in civil defense and reviving a program for building antiballistic missiles. "The United States will not accept permanent abstention from the right to protect its citizens from the effects of nuclear attack," the policy paper says.

¶ Rather than basing mutual deterrence on the capacity of nuclear weapons to kill millions of Americans and Russians, the United States should aim at military targets in the Soviet Union in time of war, not civilians.

¶ Soviet military gains in Afghanistan, or for that matter, in Eastern Europe, should not be accepted "as a permanent historical fact," according to the paper.

¶ Although the United States, on occasions, must depend on the military capabilities of allied countries to deter the Soviets, "the availability of allied support should not constrain American action in defense of its interests."

These are general guidelines, and it will take a few years to see whether a Reagan administration has made any progress in applying them. In the meantime, Reagan and his defense team will confront a host of more pressing, concrete military issues. Easily the most controversial (and costly) defense decision taken by Jimmy Carter was his approval of the MX mobile missile. Under the Carter plan, some 200 of the huge rockets, each equipped with ten multiple nuclear warheads, would be moved on giant trucks along a maze of roads to be built in remote sections of Utah and Nevada. Interspersed along the roads would be 400 to 500 concrete shelters that could be used to fire the missiles. With each of the 200 MX missiles either on the move or hidden within one of the concrete shelters, Moscow would be unable to pinpoint the location of the entire missile force and would thus be frustrated, in any crisis, from attempting a "first strike" attack. The Air Force wants to begin deploying the first MX missile by 1986, but the system is already under heavy attack from experts who claim it is unworkable as well as from local residents in Utah and Nevada who worry about its impact on the environment.

Van Cleave and other senior Reagan defense aides fully support a program for building the new MX missile, particularly because the warheads aboard the rocket would be accurate enough to destroy Soviet land-based missiles. But they assert that the Air Force's existing system of Minuteman missiles is already vulnerable to attack and thus the United States cannot wait until the end of the decade for the MX to be deployed.

In a book published last year, *Strategic Options for the Early Eighties: What Can Be Done,* Van Cleave and W. Scott Thompson, another Reagan defense adviser, maintained that "objective analyses show clearly that by the early 1980s, overall Soviet strategic nuclear force capabilities will be superior to those of the United States. Of even greater concern is that these analyses show a substantial disparity in favor of the USSR in the ability to fight, survive, win, and recover from nuclear war." Consequently, the authors advocated a series of "quick fixes" for the nation's ever-more-vulnerable strategic arsenal.

Many of the ideas proposed by Van Cleave and Thompson have been blessed by Reagan and are now being actively discussed within the Pentagon. While moving ahead with the MX, the Air Force is examining the possibility of putting a few hundred of the Air Force's existing Minuteman missiles on trucks and moving them around a series of underground shelters. Worried about the growing vulnerability (to Soviet sub-launched rockets) of the Air Force's B-52 bombers at airbases along the East and West coasts, proposals for moving the planes to bases within the nation's interior are also being studied. So too are a number of schemes for increasing the production of new air-launched cruise missiles, starting a program for a new manned bomber, and building antiballistic missile sites around key military installations around the country, such as missile bases.

In the area of conventional air, sea, and ground forces, the Reagan experts have taken aim on the so-called one-and-a-half war strategy adopted a decade ago by Richard Nixon and perpetuated by Jimmy Carter. Under the strategy, the United States is required to possess sufficient forces for fighting a full-scale conflict with the Soviet Union in Europe and extra troops for a smaller, "brush fire" war somewhere in the Third World. But the Reagan team believes that in the 1980s, the United States could find itself fighting wars in a number of areas simultaneously — Europe, the Persian Gulf, East Asia, and closer to home in the Caribbean and Central America. Accordingly, some Reagan advisers, such as Ray Klein of the Georgetown Center for Strategic and International Studies in Washington, have called for an expanded system of Western alliances, including NATO, the Far East, Australia, and others, which would give Washington and like-minded nations the ability to cope with military threats on a global front.

Such an alliance is a long way off, and in the short run Reagan and his advisers have stressed that the United States bears the primary responsibility for keeping the peace, particularly in volatile Third World regions. Thus, they are highly critical of Carter's decision to base a rapid deployment force for use in the Third World on existing forces, arguing that this is merely an exercise in "robbing Peter to pay Paul." Instead, in a report prepared for Reagan last summer, a Republican task force concluded that a massive increase in conventional strength was necessary to enable the United States "to be able to confront the new and greatly expanded Soviet ability to launch forces in important areas not now defended by the United States and its allies."

The task force, headed by retired General Edward Rowny, a former military representative in arms talks with Moscow, said that the nation needed 200 additional warships, five new Army divisions, and nine more tactical air squadrons. The report did not say how much these additional forces would cost, but a similar study prepared in 1979 by the Committee for the Present Danger, a private group with close links to Reagan, said that over the next five years, the Pentagon would need $200 billion more than spending estimates approved by the Carter administration.

The question, of course, is where the money for new strategic and conventional forces will come from. The Reagan team's sensitivity to this question was illustrated toward the end of the campaign when Van Cleave told reporters that the government had to consider the possibility of spending as much as 7 percent of the country's gross national product for defense. (A little less than 5 percent of the GNP now goes for defense.) When told about Van Cleave's remark, William Casey, Reagan's campaign chairman, quickly announced that he was not speaking for Reagan. But most military specialists around Reagan privately acknowledge that Van Cleave is probably right; in order to meet the military goals spelled out in the campaign, it will be necessary to up the defense budgets by tens of billions of dollars in future years.

One clear obstacle to boosting the defense budget is the determination of Reagan's economic advisers to bring government spending under control. Although men like Caspar Weinberger and William Simon have said that military spending must increase, there is almost certainly a gap between how they think the nation can afford it and the figures thought necessary by Reagan's defense team. Political realities must also be taken into account: as much as the conservatives around Reagan would like to cut back government's role in providing educational, health, and other services, the most pragmatic of them admit that the best that can probably be done is to limit further spending increases.

But even if the economic advisers are able to come up with a magic formula that would permit military spending to rise substantially, any new resources for defense will most likely have to go for manpower rather than new weapons and new units. This is because, by most accounts, the country's all-volunteer armed forces are failing. Instituted by Richard Nixon in the last days of the Vietnam War, the all-volunteer system is now faced with a number of seemingly insoluble problems. In the active forces, the problem is one of quality, and it is getting worse: in 1975, Army statistics show that 32 percent of new volunteers were below the national average in mental ability; in 1979, almost 60 percent were in this category. In the reserve forces, the problem is one of recruitment: the existing strength of the nation's Ready Reserve is less than 400,000, about 275,000 short of the number that Congress has approved and the Pentagon says it needs.

If the problem of recruiting people to the armed services is serious, the problem of retaining them is even worse. In the Marine Corps, for example, less than 10 percent of recruits now sign on for another tour. The Navy, meanwhile, says it needs more than 20,000 experienced chief petty officers and only has 65 percent of the number of pilots it requires for its aircraft carriers.

The Republicans are not oblivious to this situation, and Senator John Tower, the new chairman of the Armed Services Committee, told a press conference in November that dealing with the manpower dilemma would be his "first priority." The answer is simple: money. General Rowny, in a report for Reagan during the campaign, urged a 17 percent pay increase for officers and enlisted men alike. He also called on Reagan to reinstitute the educational benefits contained in the G.I. Bill and said that military pay should be indexed so that, for example, if prices went up by 10 percent, military salaries would rise by the same amount.

The problem of sorting out military priorities between manpower and additional forces is clearly a difficult one. But even if Reagan and his defense advisers are able to find a balance, they must still face other excruciating choices. One of the most difficult is whether, in buying new forces, the Pentagon should emphasize nuclear or conventional weapons. In the 1950s, the Eisenhower administration, operating under the philosophy of buying "more bang for the buck," opted for building up the country's nuclear arsenal. During the Kennedy period, this strategy was reversed, and under the "flexible response" doctrine the Pentagon was ordered to build up conventional defenses.

In much the same way, the Carter administration emphasized the importance of non-nuclear forces and launched a drive in 1977, to improve land and air forces in Western Europe. Now, a Reagan administration must decide where to set its priorities. Some Reagan military thinkers, such as Van Cleave, have stressed nuclear improvements in order to reduce the potential vulnerability of missiles and bombers to surprise attack. At the same time, however, Moscow's growing capacity to threaten vital regions, such as the Persian Gulf, has led others, like General Rowny, to emphasize the need for additional land, sea, and air units. In the area of conventional forces, moreover, there are other choices. Although the major thrust behind the Carter defense program was strengthening NATO, some Republican defense thinkers believe that this emphasis was misplaced. For a start, they contend that the allied governments of Western Europe, together with Japan, must be prodded to take on a larger burden for their own defense. Speaking to an enthusiastic group on Capitol Hill just after Reagan's election, Alexander Haig, the former NATO commander, said that Japan and Western Europe no longer suffered from war-torn economies and "they are competing with us for markets at home and abroad."

At the same time, Reagan, like many of his new team, is a Californian and does not have close ties to such institutions of the East Coast "foreign policy establishment" as the Council on Foreign Relations in New York or Harvard or Yale universities. Thus, rather than focusing on Western Europe as the linchpin of American diplomacy, there are signs that Reagan is less concerned about NATO and more sensitive to security issues in other parts of the world — in the Persian Gulf, East Asia, and Latin America. This could mean that Reagan would be much more inclined to spend extra defense funds on the Navy, the most visible form of American power in the Third World, rather than on the Army, which has the major role of defending Europe.

Less clear is how Reagan and his top aides would approach the more subtle and frustrating problem of getting the most out of the defense dollar. Jeffrey Record, a former aide to Senator Sam Nunn and a Reagan defense adviser during the campaign, has argued that the Iranian rescue fiasco offered vivid testimony to the fact that "the United States has fumbled every significant military venture it has undertaken in the last twenty years." Record and other Reagan advisers maintain that the defense dilemmas facing the country are not just the product of funding shortages, but stem from deep-seated problems within the American military itself. Like other large-scale American enterprises, be it the Chrysler Corporation or Lockheed, the Defense Department, they contend, has become a bureaucratic monster in which inertia and inefficiency, rather than innovation and accountability, characterize its day-to-day operations.

Jimmy Carter's "zero-based budgeting" was meant, four years ago, to force the Pentagon to review whether the roles and missions of the four services were relevant to a new military era. In retrospect, many senior defense officials believe that this effort failed. "Our strategy and tactics are still back in the 1950s," said one Carter appointee, who asserted that bureaucratic reforms within the military were more important to improved combat capability than any budgetary increases. A report prepared for Reagan by the Heritage Foundation, a conservative think tank in Washington, struck a similar theme, saying there were "some profound doubts as to the soundness of the present structure of U.S. forces — their styles of deployment, their methods of warfare and their equipment preferences." But Reagan may have even greater difficulty than Carter in promoting organizational reforms in the Pentagon. He is said by his closest associates to have little desire to second-guess the military and is thus more inclined to let senior officers, rather than civilian specialists, decide what kind of forces the country needs to buy.

Beyond these issues is the much more sensitive question of Reagan's propensity to use military force in foreign crises. Reagan is said by his friends to believe that to deter war, the United States not only needs adequate military forces but must also demonstrate the willingness to use them. During the Carter period, he is also known to have frequently complained to associates that the Georgian suffered from "a failure of nerve" in dealing with aggression and international terrorism abroad. In the final analysis, however, Reagan has virtually no experience in having to weigh the excruciating pros and cons of ordering American troops into action; California, after all, does not have a foreign policy nor a military establishment. Reagan's closest friends maintain that in tense situations, he is anything but "trigger happy," preferring conciliation over confrontation. But they also report that there is a point beyond which he will not allow himself to be pushed. So Reagan's propensity to use military force remains very much a mystery, probably the most important mystery confronting the nation and the world.

VII

Reagan's World

Hedrick Smith

Not since the 1960 campaign of John F. Kennedy has an American presidential candidate ridden into office sounding the alarm that the United States has fallen perilously behind Russia in the arms competition. Not since the late Secretary of State John Foster Dulles has so powerful an American leader issued the warning that the United States "has been sleepwalking too long" and must now "snap out of it" to engage anew in the global cold war.

And yet whatever themes of Kennedy and Dulles two decades ago now echo in Ronald Reagan, the irony is that in the White House, the former Governor of California may emerge more as a natural counterpart to Soviet President Leonid I. Brezhnev than as a lineal descendant of any single American leader.

For Brezhnev is a personally cordial, congenial consensus-maker who climbed to power in the provinces before ruling the Kremlin, and he has presided over the most determined, costly, and successful buildup of armed strength in Russian history. Now comes Ronald Reagan, another genial, affable politician whose roots are in the midland and whose route to power has been through distant California, and he, too, has proclaimed his dedication to a massive new American military thrust that will "restore the margin of safety" for the Free World.

Obviously, there are important differences between these ideological adversaries. But there are also intriguing parallels. Like Brezhnev, Reagan enters upon national leadership as a politician whose primary concern has been domestic affairs and who is not broadly tutored in foreign policy. In the early 1970s, President Nixon sent then-Governor Reagan on goodwill tours to the Far East and Europe, just as Brezhnev was called on for ceremonial diplomatic chores before assuming real power.

Reagan has visited more than twenty countries and met such leaders as West German Chancellor Helmut Schmidt, French President Giscard d'Estaing, and British Prime Minister Margaret Thatcher. But after he won the Republican nomination last July, Reagan decided against a trip to Europe on grounds that it would take too long for him to prepare himself and because it would seem an artificial effort to make him look expert in a field where he was still an amateur. Earlier, in a television interview, he had seemed to betray a surprising gap of knowledge when he did not quickly recognize the name of the President of France. Jimmy Carter mocked Reagan with the taunt that if the Republican were elected, participants in summit meetings would have to wear name tags for his benefit.

Reagan's inexperience brings to mind the stiff awkwardness of Brezhnev encountered by European leaders a decade ago. After the late French President Georges Pompidou and West German Chancellor Willy Brandt held their first meetings with Brezhnev, it was whispered about that the Soviet leader was so insecure in diplomatic affairs that he rigidly read the script of his briefing papers and, in response to questions, resorted to what were evidently carefully rehearsed answers. Westerners complained that Brezhnev himself was too inadequately informed to sustain a genuine dialogue, an impression that has faded in the intervening years.

Born a few years apart in the early years of the twentieth century, Brezhnev and Reagan formed their world outlook many years ago and their fundamental doctrines have been little modified by the changing tides of history. Each talks in the tongue of the true believer, with unbounded faith in the homeland and its historic mission in the world and with wary suspicion toward the bluffing and devious stratagems of ideological enemies. To hear Reagan, Communism is the implacable foe; to hear Brezhnev, it is capitalism. Rhetorically, both describe the world in black-and-white terms. It is a world of allies and adversaries, patriots and villains, loyal friends and untrustworthy enemies. It is a world where complex power relationships and subtleties or shadings of neutrality are often lost or forgotten and where the vibrant nationalism of many other peoples is dimly seen or poorly understood.

In practice, however, both men have been more pragmatic, more flexible than their rhetoric suggests. Brezhnev marched Soviet troops into Czechoslovakia when he felt vital Soviet interests were at stake and into Afghanistan when, in a less vital cause, it seemed a safe bet. But with the instinctive power-conservatism of the Soviet elders who disdain recklessness and let proxies fight most of their battles, he has acted more cautiously than he sounded on other occasions — especially when confrontation with Washington loomed.

Likewise, though Reagan is untested as a leader of foreign policy, he tempered his rhetoric with realism as Governor of California. He struck compromises and made deals with political opponents, reversed campaign slogans, and swallowed what he had labeled unthinkable before he took office. In foreign affairs, he has adjusted, though not without problems, to the American diplomatic opening to China and to the agreement to relinquish ultimate control of the Panama Canal — both of which he once adamantly and vociferously opposed.

In his inexperience and his chauvinistic enthusiasms, Reagan has sometimes exhibited Dulles's readiness to go to the brink of conflict with the Russians in a test of power over what he saw at the moment as crucial issues. But he has often retreated verbally when his own impulsive comments got him too far out on a limb.

The closer his political path brought him to the White House, the more narrowly he defined the perimeter of vital American interests. And the more eager he was to assert that he is at heart a man of peace "not trigger happy . . . not warmongering" and not itching for a showdown. For in his campaign for the Presidency, Ronald Reagan fashioned a rhetoric of implied force that is not only fervent in its insistence on greater military power but also vague as to how he would employ his power as President.

In short, there are two Reagans and the tensions between them seem almost inevitably to foreshadow differences within the new administration and to arouse conflicting passions in Congress and among the public at large. Just as in the Carter administration, these conflicting presidential impulses are likely to produce shifts and lurches and inconsistencies of policy that will bedevil friend and foe alike. They make Reagan's choice of senior defense and diplomatic advisers crucial to the course of American foreign policy over the next four years, for those who are the closest and most trusted will have great influence on which of the two Reagans is dominant at critical moments of decision.

One Reagan is the rhetorical right-winger who instinctively voices wide popular disenchantment with post-war American diplomacy, who conveys the sense that the world is a dangerous and inhospitable place and utters resentment that America has retreated in the face of Soviet advances. This is the Reagan of confrontation. This Reagan strikes a responsive chord when, his voice thickening with patriotic passion, he declares, "No more Vietnams, no more Taiwans," or when he suggests periodically it is time to strike back to demonstrate that America has not become what Richard Nixon once called "a pitiful, helpless giant." This is the politician who picked hawkish foreign policy advisers for his campaign.

The other Reagan is the pragmatic practitioner of power. His statements are more circumspect, his language more carefully ambiguous and qualified. If the right-wing Reagan urges a blockade of Cuba, the pragmatic Reagan shrewdly refuses to be lured into advocating American intervention in Iran. "I am not going to rush out and wave a blood-soaked sword and yell, 'Onward men,' and I don't think it's necessary," the pragmatic Reagan remarked last summer. "You use whatever force is necessary to achieve the purpose, and I would like to feel that there wouldn't be a need for using armed force if we made it apparent that we have the will, if necessary, to do that." This is the Reagan of accommodation, who talks of a "reasonable and balanced" relationship with Russia. This Reagan leans for advice on experienced, prudent conservatives like former Treasury Secretary George Shultz, a man with ties to European leaders and the world of international trade and finance.

But whichever side of Reagan prevails at any given moment, the new President approaches the world with a basic philosophical outlook which is a throwback to the 1950s when American power was paramount and which may founder on the more complex realities of the 1980s. His is the bipolar world of the early Cold War. For Ronald Reagan, much more than for other recent American Presidents, the global power rivalry with Moscow not only animates his thinking about foreign affairs but to a great degree it is the prism through which he views the entire world. Both intellectually and temperamentally, he is ill at ease with the diffusion of power around the world and he has set out to reverse the decline of American power.

He has minced no words in declaring that the top foreign policy priority of the Reagan administration will be quickly and dramatically to rearm the United States, to remove what he sees as a grave menace to the American nuclear deterrent forces, and to use the threat of a sharp new arms spiral to try to induce the Soviet leadership to reconsider their own nuclear strategy and ultimately to negotiate on terms that Reagan considers more equitable to Washington and its Western allies. As his associates say, he and they are prepared for a long-haul effort.

Even allowing for the exaggerated hyperbole of a political campaign, Reagan's bristling anti-Soviet declarations have constantly rung with alarm. His vision of the American peril, the Western peril, is apocalyptic. "We now enter one of the most dangerous decades of Western civilization," he warned as 1980 began. Instinctively, he has drawn parallels with the Western weakness and vacillation after Hitler's invasion of Czechoslovakia on the eve of World War II, comparing Jimmmy Carter's reaction to the Soviet invasion of Afghanistan to Neville Chamberlain, the British Prime Minister whose umbrella at Munich in 1938 became a symbol of appeasement. "I believe," he said mockingly in one campaign quip, "we are seeing the same situation as when Mr. Chamberlain was tapping the cobblestones of Munich."

"World War II came about without provocation," Reagan reasoned in a more serious setting. "It came because nations were weak, not strong, in the face of aggression. Those same lessons of the past surely apply today. Firmness based on a strong defense capability is not provocative. But weakness can be provocative simply because it is tempting to a nation whose imperialist ambitions are virtually unlimited. We find ourselves increasingly in a position of dangerous isolation. Our allies are losing confidence in us, and our adversaries no longer respect us."

Like others, Reagan has found "a threatening pattern" in the Soviet thrust into Afghanistan; in the Soviet and Cuban involvement in Marxist takeovers in Ethiopia, Angola, and South Yemen; and in Cuban-backed terrorism and upheavals around the Caribbean basin. It is Reagan's lament that "all over the world, we can see that in the face of declining American power, the Soviets and their friends are advancing."

In Africa, in Asia, in the Middle East, he clearly sees the Soviet hand behind the tumult of change. "Let us not delude ourselves," he said in a candidly revealing comment to *The Wall Street Journal*, "the Soviet Union underlies all the unrest that is going on. If they weren't engaged in this game of dominoes, there wouldn't be any hot spots in the world."

That one characteristically sweeping judgment betrayed an ignorance of, or a lack of concern for, the home-grown roots and nationalistic dynamics of the upheaval in Iran, the Arab-Israeli conflict, unrest in Southern Africa, tension in Turkey, or terrorism in Ireland, much less the broader economic confrontation between the underdeveloped raw material nations of the Southern Hemisphere and the industrialized developed nations of the North. In Reagan's scheme of things, the explosive diversity and turbulence of the Third World, the clamorous and conflicting currents running through the arc of crisis south of the Eurasian heartland and independent of Soviet adventurism are essentially unaccounted for. Nations are judged pro or con by which side they take in the global chess game, by whether they are market economies or Marxist governments. Situations are assessed by whether the cause of freedom is on the march or in retreat.

It was characteristic of Reagan, for example, to take the political risks of stirring up sharp divisions among the American electorate, by proclaiming last August that the war in Vietnam was a "noble cause." Up to that point Vietnam was a dead issue in the campaign, but Reagan felt so strongly that it was a battle for freedom and that justice was on America's side that he spoke out. His strong implication was that victory would have been possible if "our government" had applied all the means of power at its disposal to back American troops and had not been "afraid to let them win." And failure of will by American leaders is a persistent element of Reagan's critique of American foreign policy in the past quarter of a century.

Taiwan was unconscionably dumped, he said, Europe hopelessly confused by Carter's policy zig-zags, and the Shah of Iran unceremoniously abandoned. However careful Reagan was in his policy pronouncements about the ticklish hostage situation in Iran, he consistently contended that the American humiliation could have been avoided by sticking with the Shah. The calamity was caused, he argued, when President Carter "pulled the rug out from under our ally of thirty-some-odd years standing. All he had to do was stand up and stand beside the Shah's government and there wouldn't have been a successful revolution."

Steadfastness to allies has been a staple of Reagan's stump appearances. He talks as if the disarray in the Western alliance were caused simply by the failure of American will and leadership which allowed the Soviets to exploit rifts among the allies. He glosses over the increased power and determined independence of the Europeans and thinks almost exclusively in terms of American primacy in the alliance. As a consequence, he seems to believe that most alliance problems will be resolved and that Europeans will willingly come under the umbrella of American leadership once again if Washington only rectifies the strategic balance, demonstrates global firmness, and provides constancy of direction for allied policy.

"We must be the arsenal for democracy," he will say, harking back to the years before World War II when Franklin Delano Roosevelt, his early hero, used that as his battle cry to mobilize popular support for war against Nazi Germany. And with nostalgia for an earlier era of Pax Americana, Reagan goes on to add: "We did not seek leadership of the Free World, but there is no one else who can provide it, and without our leadership there will be no peace in the world."

That same prideful instinct has caused Reagan to seethe inwardly over what he sees as humiliations endured by this nation and its citizens in recent years and to assert repeatedly that America must react more forcefully to protect its interests and its people around the world. For all his frustrations, America is still a beacon to other peoples and the world is still an arena where American power, American technology, American values, the American example can make a telling difference if American leaders will only be bold enough. One of his fondest memories, Reagan told one interviewer, was seeing a newsreel of the Spanish Civil War when an American naval company went "through the streets at double-time" to an American legation in a Spanish coastal city to rescue American citizens trapped by fighting. "You couldn't help but thrill with pride at that," he said. So much was America respected, according to Reagan, that the fighting in that region was temporarily suspended to let the American rescue mission proceed.

Elsewhere, Reagan may be less prone to commit American military force than his critics fear. In the campaign, President Carter exaggerated Reagan's penchant for issuing ultimatums in his effort to paint the Californian as a reckless cowboy packing a six-gun and ready for a shootout at the least provocation. In a number of statements cited out of context by Carter, Reagan was actually advocating the use of American forces for peace-keeping purposes — in Cyprus, Lebanon, and Rhodesia.

But on other occasions, Reagan was ready — at least rhetorically — to risk actual conflict in defense of American interests. In 1975, when Ecuador seized American tuna boats for fishing inside what it claimed were its 200-mile territorial waters, Reagan proposed sending a protective Navy destroyer with the tuna boats "to cruise, say, thirteen miles offshore of Ecuador in an updated version of Teddy Roosevelt's dictum to talk softly but carry a big stick." More menacingly, in 1968 when North Korea seized the American intelligence ship *Pueblo,* Reagan declared that the American response should have been: "Send our ship and our men out within six hours or we're coming in to get them, and we'll use planes, guns, torpedoes, whatever it takes." More recently, he suggested that America could have blockaded North Korea's ports.

In 1976, during the Angolan civil war when East and West were supplying rival factions, Reagan said more vaguely that it was "time to eyeball it with Russia and the place to start is in Angola." He may have meant only sending covert aid and supplies. Just as Carter sent aircraft to Saudi Arabia in 1979 and 1980 as a show of force to bolster nervous friends on the Arabian Peninsula and the Persian Gulf, Reagan advocated an American military presence in Sinai and Pakistan after the Soviet invasion of Afghanistan. After the American hostages were seized in Iran, he sounded a blunt — though vague — warning: "What you say in a situation of that kind — and you don't say it in newspapers — you say it directly to them, 'We want our people back and we want them back today or the results are going to be very unpleasant.' "

But his most risky and controversial advocacy of the use of force was his persistent call for a naval blockade of Cuba in reprisal for the Soviet invasion of Afghanistan. "My own belief is that in addition to showing the flag there in the Middle East to indicate they might face a confrontation with us," Reagan said in the heat of the New Hampshire primary campaign last February, "we should have a plan of touching them on soft spots — for example, the suggestion I've made about blockading Cuba." Despite the contention of his then-rival, now Vice-President, George Bush, that a full blockade of Cuba would be terribly costly and perhaps impossible to impose without risking a clash with the Russians, Reagan insisted that he was "not talking about war . . . not being a warmonger. Why couldn't we blockade Cuba and then say to them, 'When your troops get out of Afghanistan, we will drop the blockade around Cuba?' " he said. "And I think this could exert great pressure. . . . I don't think they could stand a blockade very long, and I think a little call on the hot line with this kind of threat might get the withdrawal of the troops from Afghanistan."

For all his alarms about growing Soviet military superiority, he contended — somewhat inconsistently and without offering any evidence — that Moscow would back down in a crunch. The Moscow that was so menacing in his rhetoric was deemed surprisingly malleable in reality. "I don't think the Soviet Union has enough of an edge that they want a confrontation," Reagan asserted.

Much of what Reagan has been saying for years now mirrors the mood of America. During the Carter tenure, the public, the Congress, and the administration itself went through a watershed change, shifting gradually out of the neo-isolationism and the near-crippling sense of national culpability that followed the Vietnam War. Opinion polls began showing majorities in favor of higher defense spending. The public, jolted by the Iranian revolution, the threat to Western oil supplies, and the Soviet invasion of Afghanistan, seemed ready for a new era of greater American involvement in the world.

Jimmy Carter abandoned his talk of cutting the Pentagon budget and pulling ground forces out of South Korea. Instead, he began pushing for bigger defense budgets and formation of a rapid deployment force to cope with crises abroad. Negotiations were opened with Oman, Kenya, and Somalia for new American base facilities around the rim of the Indian Ocean. A new, more assertive nuclear targeting strategy was proclaimed. Audiences cheered and leapt to their feet, clapping and eyes ablaze, when Reagan declared that it was time the White House realized "we don't care whether we are liked by the rest of the world — we want to be respected."

But as Reagan takes office, he faces serious limits on American power abroad and on his own power and flexibility as President, at home as well as abroad. Republican gains in Congress last November, and especially Republican control of the Senate, assure him a more hospitable climate on Capitol Hill for his foreign and defense policies. But a sizable body of Democrats in the House is still ready to do battle to keep Reagan's drive for improved national defense from cutting too deeply into domestic programs. His opening bids for bipartisan support of his foreign policy will help him. But with a narrow balance in the Senate, Reagan may not escape the pinch of senatorial opposition to levels of aid or the supply of weapons or nuclear fuel to friendly nations abroad that has curtailed other Presidents. More broadly, the widespread public concern during the campaign about excessive interventionism abroad indicates that an uneasy public may be a restraining factor.

Abroad, Reagan faces a much more intractable world than the one idealized in his campaign speeches. It is not merely Soviet military strength that sets limits for his policies but the economic power of Europe and Japan, oil dependency in the Middle East, and the weakness of the American economy. The complexities of the strategic triangle, the Western alliance, and the Third World do not yield readily to the neat, black-and-white categories of his geopolitical checkerboard. Allies in Europe and elsewhere see his overarching anti-Communism as antiquated and counterproductive. China, the OPEC powers, Western Europeans, and others have economic and political leverage to use on Washington that will not yield to greater American military power. And they are not, as Reagan has suggested, playing some Soviet game, but acting in their own interests. Almost everywhere, Reagan's nostalgic ideological impulses are bound to bump into contemporary realities that he has overlooked or cast aside and that now stand like rocks in his path.

Given Reagan's lack of record in foreign affairs, it is impossible to predict his foreign policy with precision. Philosophically, he has laid the groundwork for radical departures from the policies of President Carter. He has opposed détente, Salt II, and the return of the Panama Canal to Panama. He believes that a stepped-up arms race can lead to arms reduction ultimately. His rumbling rhetoric about the use of force and his recollection of the Vietnam War as "a noble cause" seem to foreshadow an aggressive policy in the Third World. Indeed, there and toward Moscow, he will take a new tack. But in other areas his course may not diverge so dramatically from Carter's as both of them made it sound during the campaign. He'll have to trim his sails to realities.

"I would not foresee radical policy shifts in the Reagan administration," said Richard V. Allen, his top foreign policy adviser in the campaign, sounding the pragmatic theme for Reagan. "There are sobering realities that confront a President on January 21st. We do not control events. All we can do is shape them."

In one classic case, Reagan had to shift to the Carter course in the midst of his own campaign: toward China. That country is a prototype of situations where Reagan's over-hasty and outdated ideological reflexes have gotten him into trouble and he has had to change position. With greater pragmatism than he is usually given credit for, Reagan had long before muted his outspoken anti-Communist rhetoric toward China and his long-held suspicion of the Peking regime, in good part because he began to see China as a potential partner in the three-cornered strategic poker game with the Soviet Union. With the Republican nomination in hand last July, he began espousing broader relations with China and sent his running mate, George Bush, on a goodwill mission to

Peking designed to earn points with the electorate for the sensitive and moderate approach of a Reagan administration.

Instead, the rhetorical Reagan torpedoed the pragmatic Reagan's mission before it was launched by getting snarled up in one of his pet ideological attachments: Taiwan. In December 1978, the Carter administration had agreed to have the United States represented in Taiwan by a private foundation, staffed by American diplomats, but Reagan, an ardent friend of Taiwan, had been outraged to see an old ally treated this way. Campaigning in May he had declared that if elected, he would seek to re-establish "official relations" with Taiwan, which he called "the true Republic of China." Despite his parallel interest in broadening ties with Peking, the Chinese were angered by his resurrection of the Taiwan issue. Reagan, bellowed the Peking *People's Daily,* intends to turn the clock back and conduct American foreign policy as if there were two Chinas. It will be very dangerous."

The candidate himself raced off to other matters closer to home while Allen tried to repair the damage and brush the whole controversy under the rug. Allen, who is more attuned than Reagan to the nuances of diplomacy, the terms of the American-Chinese diplomatic agreement, and the technicalities of the Taiwan Relations Act expressing congressional approval for unofficial relations, insisted in July that Reagan had given up the idea of resuming "official relations" with Taiwan. He did not intend to alter the status quo, Allen said.

Yet as Bush was preparing to board his plane to China, Reagan revived the thorny issue of "official relations" with Taiwan at an airport news conference in Los Angeles on August 18. As Bush winged his way across the Pacific, Peking admonished Reagan for a "brazen" and "absurd" position that "would in fact destroy the basic principle of normalization of U.S.-China relations and surely affect normalization between the two countries." In other words, chose them or us, Peking was telling Reagan.

For several awkward days, while Bush was eating long Chinese dinners in Peking and trying to reassure his Chinese hosts that the Reagan administration did not intend to change the accepted terms of relations, Reagan continued clumsily to sow confusion back in America. Once again, he came out for "official government relations" with Taiwan. As Bush departed from Peking, the Chinese gave him a parting blast, saying his mission had "failed to reassure China" about Reagan's intentions.

Back in California, the two Republicans held a news conference on August 25 in which the rhetorical, right-wing Reagan had to bow to reality — China was more important than Taiwan and the die had already been cast. He conceded past misstatements and pointedly dropped his insistence on "official relations" with Taiwan. With some justification, Reagan contended that since the American Institute in Taiwan was so heavily staffed by American diplomats, it was transparently "hypocritical" to pretend that this was an "unofficial" agency — though that is what he himself had previously been saying. But from now on, Reagan said, he would regard the institute as official in reality if not in name.

For Reagan, that ended the episode. The pragmatic Reagan has since reaffirmed, more stoutly than ever, his desire to promote the "rapid growth" of American ties with China, though he left rather vague whether this meant making available some military equipment and coordinating strategies to contain the Soviet Union as well as boosting trade and cultural exchanges. Whatever the intent, he sounded very much in harmony with Carter policy as he approached his election. Nonetheless, Reagan is now handicapped. Peking continues to sputter and fume. As President, Reagan begins his tenure with a fresh legacy of mistrust to overcome in Peking because of his own clumsiness.

The entire episode may be symptomatic of the kind of difficulty Reagan may encounter with other major world powers — for example, in Europe — because of his relative inexperience and his insensitivity to the changes of the past decade or two. His impulse to shore up the alliance parallels Carter's basic approach. But if the former Governor of Georgia never won lasting respect from European leaders because he failed to appreciate adequately their independent-minded views, Reagan may compound that problem.

"There's a generation gap between what Reagan thinks he knows about the world and the reality," observes John Sears, the Washington attorney who managed Reagan's 1976 campaign and did it again in 1980 until he was dismissed early in the year. "His is a kind of 1952 world. He sees the world in black and white terms. That's okay if he has the right Secretary of State and the right National Security Adviser. The dangerous thing is not the Russians, but other situations beyond the Russians. Reagan's going to be upset to find out that some countries in Western Europe part company with us rather sharply on a number of issues. He tends to assume a community of both objectives and tactics, that all want, at bottom, to 'beat the Russians.' "

Dealing with the alliance powers will prove a major test of Reagan's adaptability. For coming into office, he seemed not to have fathomed how much American influence in the alliance has diminished as a natural consequence of European resurgence. His own perspective bears the hallmark of a simpler era when American power was so preeminent that Washington's decisions set the course for NATO. Now, for all his talk of improving alliance cooperation, he conveys an implicit, underlying go-it-alone American philosophy that assumes that if America only shows forceful leadership, loyal allies will naturally follow.

In Reagan's rather wistful view, America's current difficulties with its major allies are traceable to erratic Carter leadership and strategic slippage in the competition with Moscow. Carter caused confusion, Reagan has argued, by pushing a neutron warhead for the European theater and then backtracking once the Germans were ready to go along. His implication is that wider harmony can be restored by pressing ahead with a neutron warhead: never mind divisions among European nations on this issue or the public opposition that plagues even some of those governments ready to move ahead. Reagan's stress on military preparedness will boost morale, no doubt, in some quarters of Europe. But his hardline talk of standing against the Russians already has other Europeans nervous. The lesson lies ahead that alliance leadership requires more than a certain trumpet.

Reagan used the first press conference after his election to reassure the allies and to proclaim the importance of the Europeans and his desire for "very close" relations with France, among others. But in the simplistic symmetry of his bipolar world he has shown little comprehension that European leaders such as President Giscard d'Estaing of France see a positive virtue in a strong, independent Europe able to deal with the United States on equal footing and to conduct its own affairs with the Russians, rather than having Washington speak for a united West. With Europe resurgent, economic rivalries and centrifugal forces divide the Western powers, apart from any Soviet chicanery or shortfalls in the Western arsenal. If Reagan treats Europe as an off-shoot of the Soviet-American relationship, he is in for trouble.

During the campaign, for example, when European leaders were balking at President Carter's retaliatory grain embargo against the Russians, Reagan was complaining that the action was too mild. What the rhetorical Reagan advocated was a complete, across-the-board trade boycott, showing little comprehension that the Germans, French, and other continental powers have little taste for confrontation with Moscow over Afghanistan because they have a far greater economic stake in détente than America. If Reagan follows his historic right-wing impulses to face down the Russians, he is likely to be left out on a limb with little meaningful support from the alliance. Here, as with China, the pragmatic Reagan is likely to have to make adjustments.

Obviously foreshadowing the difficulties ahead, Senator Howard Baker of Tennessee issued a report after a trip to Europe in August declaring that a unified Western response to Afghanistan had been hampered by "a substantially different interpretation of détente in Europe from that of the most prudent observers in the United States." Baker — hardly noted for extremism — said he had found a "fundamental disagreement over the character of the political and military policies required for the conduct of stable East-West relations." In concrete terms, this meant that at a time when Reagan's experts were talking about an increase of 7-to-9 percent in the military budget (a real increase, after inflation), Chancellor Schmidt was saying that West Germany's economic problems might keep it from meeting the allowance goal of raising defense spending by 3 percent a year.

Not only economic rivalries but differing approaches to the common need for imported energy drive perplexing wedges in the alliance, and so far Reagan has shown little appreciation of how Europe and America diverge on this issue. The Europeans, feeling far more dependent on Middle East oil and hence much more vulnerable than America to another Arab oil embargo or cutoff arising from a regional war, have taken a different tack in their diplomacy, and may wind up differing more sharply with Reagan than with Jimmy Carter.

Optimistically, both Reagan and the Republican platform talk of working to revive the North Atlantic Treaty Organization and perhaps to extend its arm of protection into such strategic regions as the Indian Ocean. The Iraqi war with Iran, which stirred a common Western impulse to protect the vital flow of oil through the Persian Gulf and the Straits of Hormuz, may have provided an opening for the kind of collaboration a Reagan administration would like to pursue.

Skillful diplomacy may succeed. But if the Reagan team pushes for rapid construction of a new architecture of regional alliances, reminiscent of the 1950s, they face reluctant partners in Europe. Except in the most acute situations — and they are usually temporary — European leaders do not share what has come across to them as Reagan's inclination to draw lines in the sand against Russians or others who threaten Western interests. Rather than sharing Reagan's rhetorical inclination to threaten force, the Europeans have favored intricate peace diplomacy sympathetic to the Palestinians that may put them on a collision course with Reagan. For the Europeans have looked for some time to an equitable

Arab-Israeli peace agreement as the best long-term guarantee of a steady supply of Middle East oil to the West.

The Third World is one of two areas (the Soviet Union is the other) where Reagan's policies will probably diverge most noticeably from the Carter years. Although Carter warned Americans that Reagan is "trigger-happy" and prone to use force, that may not be Reagan's main problem in the most turbulent regions of the Third World. Reagan is a self-confident man, not one plagued by the kind of personal insecurities that would prompt him as President into a macho display of power to prove himself. Some who have known him for a long time, like John Sears, do not believe that he will be as reckless or as aggressive as his right-wing rhetoric has made him sound.

In the one Third World crisis that persisted during the campaign, Reagan was very restrained about the use of American power. He was less venturesome than President Carter, who warned in his State of the Union Address last January that America was ready to use any means, including force, to repel an outside attempt to control the Persian Gulf. In San Francisco last May, Reagan was asked whether he would send Moscow "a clear-cut ultimatum not to meddle" in Iran or risk American counteraction. His reply was to raise a cautionary theme he sounded several more times in the campaign: America was not strong enough or positioned well enough to make such a threat.

"We could send an ultimatum but what would we back it up with?" he asked. Russia, he contended, has 150,000 troops poised on the Iranian border, far outgunning the Americans. "Logistically, we're talking about thousands and thousands of miles from our borders," he said. "Maybe the signal [against Soviet intervention] we should send should be a bit further back, and that might be Saudi Arabia. And if we send it, we should send it only with the collaboration of our allies, Japan and Europe, who are so dependent on OPEC oil." Such comments caused former Secretary of State Henry Kissinger to observe much later, "Recklessness will be the least of Reagan's problems."

A more likely pitfall for Reagan is his ignorance of the complex forces that boil over unpredictably in the Third World and his reflexive instinct to categorize nations as friend or foe and base his diplomacy on that single judgment. In the Reagan years, Carter's vocal concern for human rights, the North-South dialogue, and nuclear proliferation will be replaced by a more focused and exclusive effort to build up right-wing regional partners in the strategic rivalry with Moscow and to apply pressure against partisans of the other side.

A Reagan administration is likely to move toward more clear-cut and untroubled relations with allies such as South Korea and the Philippines. But conversely, the rhetorical Reagan's penchant for ideological judgments may not only alienate left-leaning non-aligned states such as India and Iraq and shut the door to ultimate accommodation with Marxist regimes in Angola and Nicaragua, but it may even trouble hesitant friends such as Pakistan, Saudi Arabia, and Jordan, who nervously vacillate about how visibly they want American support or whether they would like an American military presence on their territory.

Reagan's urge toward steadfastness to friends in Asia, Africa, and Latin America sometimes carries with it a noticeable naiveté about the world and betrays Reagan's inexperience or lack of sophistication about frictions among American friends abroad that limit Washington's maneuvering room and force American diplomacy to tread carefully to avoid angering some would-be allies in the act of befriending others.

In the Middle East, where Carter tried to strike a balance, Reagan has talked enthusiastically about Israel as a strategic ally — to the delight of some and the chagrin of others. Repeatedly, he has proclaimed that American support for Israel springs not primarily from a historic special relationship or a moral obligation inherited from the Holocaust, but it rests most fundamentally on the calculation that in the global struggle, Israel is a strategic ally that can in some undefined way help secure a vital geographic region.

"Israel is the only stable democracy we can rely on in a spot where Armageddon could come," he has said. "The greatest responsibility the United States has is to preserve peace — and we need an ally in that area. We must prevent the Soviet Union from penetrating the Mideast. The Nixon administration unsuccessfully moved them out. If Israel were not there, the United States would have to be there." More concretely, Reagan has talked, for example, of forming an anti-Soviet defense alliance with Israel, Egypt, and Saudi Arabia — an adaptation of the defunct Baghdad Pact strategy of the 1950s so ardently promoted by the late John Foster Dulles. At other times, Reagan has sounded as though he would like to base American forces, more or less permanently, in Israel.

But in his friendship and support of Israel, pushed so zealously during the election campaign, he seemed oblivious to the price he would pay among the Arabs if he pursued this strategy in office. Too ardent an embrace of Israel would not only inflame the Arab radicals but offend such moderates as Saudi Arabia, the Persian Gulf emirates, and Jordan. Reagan's campaign rhetoric suggested, moreover, that he does not see the Palestinian question as an issue of fundamental consequence to the Saudis and other Arabs, and hence has failed to grasp its significance for the wider American strategy in the Middle East, either to secure oil or foil the Soviets. He may speak with admiration of President Anwar Sadat of Egypt or suggest throwing the mantle of Western protection around the Saudi monarchy. But in his eager pursuit of Jewish support in his race for the Presidency, he has given virtually unqualified endorsement to the Israeli position, breaking with established American policy by backing Israel's push for West Bank settlement and its integration of Jerusalem as its undivided capital. "An undivided city of Jersualem means sovereignty for Israel over the city," he told a delighted band of Jewish leaders in New York. "The West Bank should be a decision worked out by Jordan and Israel. I would never have supported dismantling [of Israeli settlements on the West Bank and in Jerusalem]."

Like others, Reagan has disparaged the Palestine Liberation

Organization as "a terrorist group" with ominous links to Moscow. He has also treated the Palestinian issue as a refugee problem soluble by some mechanistic mathematical formula, rather than an explosively complex political issue with wide ramifications for American relations with the Arab world, and for relations with Europe beyond. "Palestine was never a country," Reagan observed in one political debate. "It was a territory, an area, and it was a British mandate. And it was the British government that created the Kingdom of Jordan which is 80 percent of what used to be Palestine. The Israelis have less than 20 percent of what was Palestine. The Palestinian refugee problem, it seems to me then, is an 80 percent-20 percent problem of Jordan and Israel."

Without Jordan's participation in peace negotiations, that approach can hardly succeed. No sooner did he win the election than Reagan expressed an interest in meeting with King Hussein of Jordan. But his public positions are hardly enticing to Hussein. Reagan has gone further than any previous American President in disagreeing with Jordanian terms for a settlement by backing Israel's West Bank settlements and Jerusalem as Israel's capital. These views will prove a considerable handicap to any effort Reagan makes to draw the King into Arab-Israeli peace negotiations.

In the end, unless the pragmatic Reagan moderates the rhetorical Reagan's positions and launches a deliberate diplomacy to woo the moderate Arabs, the new President may even find himself hard-pressed to keep President Sadat of Egypt engaged in negotiations with Israel. For Sadat's patience has rested heavily on his personal relationship with Jimmy Carter and his faith in Carter's even-handedness between Israel and Egypt. And an open collapse of the peace process in the Middle East will invite wider violence in an already volatile region.

Somewhat belatedly, Reagan made friendly noises toward Saudi Arabia, the most important of the oil suppliers, a nation that has repeatedly resisted or moderated the sharpest OPEC price increases and boosted its oil output to help the West during the Iranian crisis. The Saudis are likely to test Reagan quickly by renewing their request for sophisticated equipment that will give offensive capability for the American-built F-15 fighters sold to them by the Carter administration.

Because Israel so vocally opposed such a sale, reminding Carter that he had promised the Senate that no such equipment would be added to the planes, he rejected the Saudi request on the virtual eve of the election. But with a new administration in office, the issue is bound to be revived and Reagan's reaction watched as a touchstone of his attitudes in office.

Elsewhere in the Third World, Reagan's ideological instincts, if carried into practice, will produce cleavages that Carter sought to avoid. In Latin America, for example, the Reagan approach will probably refurbish relations with what Reagan strategists like to call "the ABC countries" — Argentina, Brazil, and Chile — which had their frictions with the Carter administration over human rights. Conversely, it will almost certainly bring diplomatic clashes and perhaps more with Fidel Castro's Cuba and Caribbean leftists.

Reagan himself has called Latin America a touchstone for American relations with the Third World and a rising battleground with Communism. He has berated the Carter administration for ignoring realpolitik by its idealistic "bullying" of countries like Brazil and Argentina. And alarmed by what he sees as the rising leftist threat in Nicaragua, El Salvador, Guatemala, and Honduras, he has sharply chided his predecessor for aiding the leftist Sandanista government in Nicaragua. At heart, his fear is that Castro, acting as an agent for the Kremlin, is fomenting revolution and turmoil around the Caribbean, aiming to turn it into what Reagan called "a red sea" that will eventually engulf Mexico and leave the United States with a hostile, oil-rich neighbor on its southern border.

The hallmark of Reagan's own approach to Latin America for years was his relentless campaign against the treaties that will eventually turn over control of the Panama Canal to Panama. His blunt summary was: "We built it. We paid for it. It's ours, and we're going to keep it." Now that the treaties have been ratified, however, the pragmatic Reagan has grudgingly relented and raised the issue only to warn that Panama must live up to their spirit and letter.

The Republican Party platform sounded the trumpet for a battle against Caribbean leftists, but in a major foreign policy speech on October 19, Reagan himself promised to "initiate a program of intensive economic development with cooperating countries of the Caribbean." Between the lines, he seemed to differentiate between general leftists and out-and-out accessories of Castro and the Kremlin, and rather vaguely held out the prospect of financial and technical aid for those receptive to American help. Only practice will define whom that includes.

It is clear, however, that Reagan intends to pursue a progressive policy toward Mexico, not only because of its obvious size, wealth, and importance but also because, as Governor of California, he dealt personally with the issue of illegal Mexican immigrants, and as a candidate he visited Mexico and talked with President Lopez Portillo. He came home talking of a North American Accord, the one real foreign policy departure of his campaign, embracing Mexico, Canada, and the United States. What he envisioned was a tripartite council to enable the three neighbors to deal more effectively with issues arising from their interdependent economies. He also came home advocating an American open-border policy for Mexican migrant workers, sure to appeal to the kind of American agribusinesses in the Southwest who back Reagan, but also likely to relieve political tensions with Mexico. "They have a problem of 40-to-50 percent unemployment," Reagan said of Mexico. "Why don't we work out some recognition of our mutual problems, make it possible for them to come here legally with a work permit? This is the only safety valve they have right now with the unemployment, that probably [can] keep the lid from blowing off down there."

Reagan associates contend that his attitude toward Mexico is indicative of his flexibility once he gets to know a situation, preferably firsthand. He is not so ideologically rigid, they say, that he cannot work with a leftist government that presides over a mixed economy, as in Mexico, especially if there is the specter of an even more threatening swing to the far left. It is that bogeyman of Marxist extremism or the Soviet bear that may produce the most pragmatic actions of the Reagan administration in the Third World.

By far the most striking break from Carter's foreign policy appears in Reagan's approach to the Soviet Union. He has rejected "the illusion of détente," which he claims lulled the West into expecting Soviet restraint around the world and in the arms race. He has vowed to withdraw from the Senate the Strategic Arms Limitation Treaty negotiated from 1972 until 1979 and signed by Carter and Brezhnev in Vienna, as a "flawed treaty" that permits the Soviets to race ahead with their military buildup while restraining the United States and, as he and his advisers like to put it, "freeze the United States into a position of permanent inferiority." Until close to the end of his campaign, he talked the language of confrontation. Only in the waning fortnight, with the election in the balance, did Reagan stike a more pragmatic and balanced approach on both arms control and general dealings with the Russians.

But his latest positions come against the backdrop of his fervent, long-held views that "there is a Communist plan for world conquest" with the United States as the ultimate target. In his famous television speech in 1964 on behalf of Senator Barry Goldwater, then the Republican nominee, Reagan posed the global contest in stark and dramatic terms: "We are at war with the most dangerous enemy that has ever faced mankind in his long climb from the swamp to the stars, and it has been said if we lose that war, and in so doing lose this way of freedom of ours, history will record with the greatest astonishment that those who had the most to lose did the least to prevent its happening."

Western peril, he has suggested, is at its peak in the era of détente because of false expectations. "Where is the Soviet restraint promised in the Code of Détente of 1972?" the rhetorical Reagan asked last spring. "Is it visible in the Russian military buildup in

North Korea? Or in the occupied islands north of Japan? Did we see it in Hanoi's annexation of Indochina? In Soviet complicity in the starvation of the people of Cambodia? The Soviet provision of poison gas used against the hill tribesmen of Laos? Is Russian restraint evident in their military intervention with Cuban proxies in wars in Angola and Ethiopia? Is it visible in their imperial invasion of the then independent, neutral nation of Afghanistan, where they executed their own puppet president and his entire family, including even his three-year-old daughter?"

Far more unnerving in Reagan's eyes, however, has been Moscow's drive for strategic nuclear superiority which, if unchecked and unmatched, as he told the Veterans of Foreign Wars in Chicago last August, threatens the West with an ultimate choice of war or surrender. "The Soviets want peace and victory," he asserted. "They seek a superiority in military strength that, in the event of a confrontation, would leave us with an unacceptable choice between submission or conflict."

"We face a situation in which our principal adversary, the Soviet Union, surpasses us in virtually every category of military strength," he said last spring. Later, he estimated that the Soviets "lead us in all but six or eight [of the forty strategic military categories] and may well surpass us in those, if present trends continue." Over the past decade, he has argued, Moscow spent $240 billion more than Washington on defense and is now outspending America by $50 billion a year.

Such anxieties have plagued conservatives and hawks for years. But they now win a broader consensus among Washington policy-makers and reflect a more pervasive public mood. The Reagan camp can cite not only its own experts but also top military brass in the Carter administration. As Reagan reminded a national television audience on October 19, the Senate Armed Services Committee was so concerned about the trends in the arms race that it concluded in December 1979 that "the SALT II Treaty, as it now stands, is not in the national security interests of the United States of America."

Most significantly, the Reaganites were armed with the first acknowledgement from Harold R. Brown, the Carter Defense Secretary, that Soviet nuclear forces have developed sufficient capability in late 1980 that the American arsenal of 1,054 land-based missiles "could be destroyed within a very short time as one result of a Soviet surprise attack." Moreover, with Soviet capabilities improving far more rapidly than American intelligence had expected only a year or two ago, Brown contended that "at least potentially" Soviet programs would "threaten the survivability of each component of our strategic forces" — bombers and submarines as well as land-based ICBMs. Later, Brown backtracked a bit on that estimate, but Reagan's argument had already been buttressed.

The Reagan strategy is to withdraw the SALT II arms control agreement and to put pressure on the Soviet leadership to agree to an agreement more favorable to Washington by confronting the Kremlin with a major new American military surge which, as the Republican platform optimistically put it, will be "sufficient to close the gap and ultimately reach the position of military superiority." So controversial and scary is the concept of superiority to much of the American electorate that the mere mention of it revived anxious debate over the prospect of an open-ended arms race that would permanently kill all prospects for arms control. Reagan found refuge during the campaign in the ambivalent declaration that he wanted to "restore the margin of safety" for America, letting conservatives read that as superiority and moderates and liberals hope that it meant something less.

"My objection to SALT II is not arms limitation," he said in a crucial interview with The Associated Press on October 1. "It legitimizes the arms race. It begins by letting the Soviet Union build 3,000 more warheads, then we can build some to catch up, only we can't catch up until 1990. I think it is a fatally flawed treaty, and it isn't arms limitation. If we're really going to try to remove the danger to the world today, let's sit down with the intention voiced and the agreement of the other side that we're going to find a way to fairly reduce the strategic weapons [of both sides] so that neither one of us can threaten the other."

But, he insisted, the American slant on arms talks had to be different from the past. "I don't think that we should sit at the table the way we have in the past," he said. "We have been unilaterally disarming at the same time we're negotiating supposed arms limitation with the other fellow, where all he has to do is sit there and not give up anything and his superiority increases. He will be far more inclined to negotiate in good faith if he knows that the United States is engaged in building up its military. "They know our industrial strength. They know our capacity. The one card that's been missing in these negotiations has been the possibility of an arms race. Now the Soviets have been racing, but with no competition. No one else is racing. And so I think that we'd get a lot farther at the table if they know that as they continue, they're faced with our industrial capacity and all that we can do."

His objectives, he went on to say, were either to persuade the Kremlin to accept absolute arms reductions or to improve the American defense posture to the point that "once again the possibility of a [Soviet] pre-emptive strike has been eliminated." Throughout the campaign, Reagan and his aides studiously avoided putting a precise time frame and a dollar ceiling on their projected buildup. Reagan pledged simply to spend "whatever is necessary."

Despite his skittishness about budget figures, Reagan has made clear his intention to give defense spending priority not only over domestic programs but even over balancing the budget, long one of his cherished goals. By the estimates of some of his advisers, the Reagan defense budgets between now and 1985 will run at least $150 billion and perhaps about $250 billion more than the Carter administration had planned to spend.

But in Reagan's prescription, more than dollars are required. If America is to achieve what he calls "peace through strength," it must regain its will, its firmness. It must shake what he calls "the Vietnam syndrome." The lesson of that war, he contends, was not that it was mistaken or immoral but simply this: "If we are forced to fight, we must have the means and the determination to prevail or we will not have what it takes to secure the peace."

Seeking to capitalize politically on the ominous sound of the Reagan program, President Carter warned that his challenger was edging the nation toward "a nuclear precipice." Reagan, he said, was "extraordinarily naive" about the nuclear arms race and Soviet psychology and "does not understand the serious consequences of what he's proposing." From his own experience, Carter declared, it was a "naive assumption" that the Soviets' response "to all these steps will be to agree to new concessions and reductions in their nuclear arsenal." Coming from Carter, the point seemed especially well taken, for he began his administration in 1977 by setting aside the Nixon and Ford efforts toward a SALT II agreement and sending his Secretary of State, Cyrus R. Vance, to Moscow to seek significant arms reduction. Moscow objected strenuously, publicly denounced the idea, and stonily forced the Carter administration to revive the Vladivostok formula, worked out in 1974 by former President Ford, and to use that as the basis for a new arms agreement.

During the campaign, the Soviet press lampooned Reagan "as an aggressive and ignorant Californian who does not remember the name of the President of France, who mixes up North Vietnam and North Korea, and who repeatedly refers to Indonesia as Indochina. But with the realpolitik that guides Soviet thinking, the tone changed after the election. Moscow did not immediately slam the door to Reagan's approach on SALT. It was up to the new administration, the Soviets told an American delegation to Moscow in November, to propose "desired changes" in the SALT II treaty. Some of the American group were encouraged by Moscow's apparent willingness to listen. On November 17, Brezhnev made a point of treating Reagan's campaign oratory as a thing of the past, asserting that "any constructive steps" by Washington would meet with "a positive reaction on our part."

In practice, that may not turn out to be as promising as it sounds. One of the participants in the informal Soviet-American talks, Lincoln Bloomfield, an arms control specialist with long experience with the Russians, called the latest meeting "one of the

New Team: Republican nominees Ronald Reagan, with his wife Nancy, and George Bush, with his wife Barbara, tour a Houston shopping mall shortly after the Republican National Convention. *(UPI)*

OFF AND RUNNING

In Charge: Candidate Reagan holds his first staff meeting after being nominated the Republican presidential candidate. *(AP)*

With Jackson: To gain insights on problems facing blacks, Reagan meets with the Reverend Jesse Jackson at Operation Push. *(UPI)*

With GOP Leaders: A gathering of top Republicans: *(from left)* Bill Brock, GOP national chairman; Reagan; John Rhodes, House minority leader; George Bush, Republican vice-presidential nominee; and Howard Baker, Senate minority leader. *(UPI)*

With Kissinger: Reagan walks and talks with Henry Kissinger, Secretary of State under Presidents Nixon and Ford. *(UPI)*

William J. Casey: Reagan's presidential campaign director. *(Wide World)*

Richard Wirthlin: Reagan's campaign pollster and senior strategist. *(Wide World)*

James A. Baker III: George Bush's presidential campaign director, President Ford's Undersecretary of Commerce, and campaign director against Jimmy Carter in 1976. *(Wide World)*

Lyn Nofziger: An old hand from Reagan's California governorship, he joined the Reagan presidential campaign as press secretary. *(Wide World)*

Stuart Spencer: A veteran California political consultant, he played a key role in planning the Reagan victory strategy. *(Wide World)*

Dr. Martin Anderson: A fellow at the Hoover Institute at Stanford University, Anderson has been Reagan's senior domestic-affairs adviser. *(Wide World)*

Richard V. Allen: Reagan's chief foreign-policy adviser, he served on the Nixon administration's National Security Council. Charges that he had profited from that office led to his withdrawal from the campaign toward the end, though Reagan expressed full confidence in him. He was a senior adviser on the transition team. *(Wide World)*

Edwin Meese III: He won a power struggle with John P. Sears and emerged as the campaign's chief of staff. He holds a newly created Cabinet level post, Counselor to the President. *(Wide World)*

John P. Sears *(left):* Reagan's chief of staff in the 1976 presidential campaign and again in 1980 until he lost out to Edwin Meese. Sears discovered that Reagan was prepared to be quite unconventional—to the discomfort of more conservative Republicans. Senator Paul Laxalt *(right):* A longtime Reagan friend and political counselor, he was reelected to the Senate as a Republican from Nevada. *(Wide World)*

Arthur F. Burns *(left)*: Chairman of the Federal Reserve Board during the Nixon and Ford years and part of the Carter administration. *(Wide World)*

Milton Friedman *(right):* Professor of economics at the University of Chicago and a Nobel laureate. *(UPI)*

Charls E. Walker *(left):* Former Deputy Secretary of the Treasury and chief tax adviser to Reagan. *(AP)*

Arthur Laffer *(right):* Professor of economics at the University of Southern California, supply-side champion, and originator of the "Laffer curve." *(AP)*

(Above) Senator William Roth (left), Republican from Delaware, and Representative Jack Kemp (right), Republican from New York, are the authors of a bill that would curb Federal spending and cut income taxes by 30 percent over the next three years. (UPI)·

George Shultz: The former Secretary of the Treasury was a senior adviser to Reagan. (UPI)

THE CAMPAIGN TRAIL

Rough Going: As Reagan campaigns at a steel plant in Youngstown, Ohio, he passes a Carter poster. *(AP)*

Easy Going: Toward the campaign's end, Reagan is greeting by scores of supporters in Florida. *(AP)*

Off the Beaten Track: A very private couple, the Reagans relax at their isolated ranch near Santa Barbara before heading into the campaign. *(UPI)*

Plane Strategy: Reagan hears out adviser Alan Greenspan *(left)* on the candidate's major economic speech while adviser Martin Anderson listens. *(UPI)*

Debate Strategy: Reagan plans for the nationally televised debate against President Carter with advisers Richard Wirthlin *(back to camera)* and William Simon. *(AP)*

Face-to-Face: President Carter and Reagan greet each other on stage before their only campaign debate. Reagan was generally considered to have scored well against Carter, a high-water mark for him in the campaign. *(UPI)*

ELECTION DAY 1980

To the Polls: Independent candidate John Anderson prepares to vote in his hometown of Rockford, Illinois. Anderson's third-party candidacy did not seriously affect the outcome of the election. *(UPI)*

A Confident Voter: A casual Ronald Reagan picks up his ballot on Election Day. *(UPI)*

Carter Loses: President Carter concedes defeat early in the evening of Election Day. With him are his wife Rosalynn, daughter Amy, and grandson Jason. *(UPI)*

Sad News: At what would have been his victory celebration, President Carter is consoled by his staff and his cabinet officers and their wives. *(UPI)*

VICTORY!

Winning Team: President-elect Ronald Reagan and Vice-President-elect George Bush at their first news conference, November 7. *(AP)*

Reagan Takes the Cake: The map on the Reagan victory cake, with flags marking the states he won, indicates the Reagan landslide. *(AP)*

Many Happy Returns: President-elect Reagan and wife Nancy enjoy a congratulatory call on election night. *(AP)*

New President and First Lady: President-elect Reagan and wife Nancy greet well-wishers after church on the Sunday after his election. *(AP)*

most sober I ever experienced. I thought they [the Soviets] were quite pessimistic in their evaluations of the period ahead."

Whatever is now said in public, Reagan brooks the disfavor of the Soviet leadership by rejecting an arms agreement negotiated by two previous Presidents. More fundamentally, having achieved at least rough strategic parity with America through an eighteen-year arms buildup, the Soviet leaders are unlikely to let it slip now from their grasp. Their arms programs have developed momentum, far more momentum than the American experts anticipated only a few years ago. And it took long, arduous bargaining for them to accept the agreement that Reagan believes is to their advantage, making it highly unlikely that they will accede any time soon to what he obviously intends as his advantageous terms.

Another complication arose in Reagan's first comments after the election when he said he would link arms negotiations with Soviet behavior around the world. "I believe in linkage," he said, reviving a Nixon-era concept abandoned by the Carter administration. "The policies of aggression of the Soviet Union . . . must be a part of discussions and negotiations that go forward," he said. "I don't think you simply sit down at the table to discuss arms limitations, for example, but you discuss the whole attitude, world attitude, as to whether we're going to have a world of peace or whether we're simply going to talk about weaponry and not bring up these other subjects." To *Time* magazine, he suggested that if Moscow did not like the idea that "their overall policy of aggression must be a part of what is going on at the negotiating table . . . maybe the disadvantage [to them] would be that you wouldn't negotiate."

The hard Reagan line, coming at a time of Soviet transition to new leadership, may spur yet another Soviet effort to repair relations with China and prompt new Soviet stratagems to split off America from West Europeans who have come to regard arms control agreements as a reassuring foundation for détente.

Sensing nervousness about his approach, the pragmatic Reagan sought to calm an anxious American electorate with his promise on October 19 to "begin immediate preparations for negotiations on a SALT III treaty." He replaced some of his own bristling rhetoric with the assertion that "we seek neither confrontation nor conflict" and the conviction that "with our allies, we can conduct a realistic and balanced policy toward the Soviet Union." And in his first post-election press conference, he was more positive than previously about SALT II. He suggested that it not be rejected out of hand but that the two sides "take what is usable out of SALT II" as the basis for renewed discussions or as an interim agreement, while they seek significant reductions in SALT III.

But if his approach was sounding more pragmatic, his logic had not altered. He remains convinced that the leverage of American industrial might, technological ingenuity, and economic flexibility will ultimately cause the Kremlin to reconsider and raise its own policies as it faces the prospect of being outrun in a new arms race of the 1980s as it was in the moon race of the 1960s. He has been told by his advisers that the Soviet leaders have already squeezed their consumers and their economy to the limit so that he believes there is no real slack in the Soviet economy to throw more resources into an accelerated arms competition.

"I don't know whether the Soviets will ever sincerely share our aspirations for strategic stability, and our desire to reduce nuclear armaments," Reagan said late last summer. "I don't know whether they will ever be willing to moderate arms competition in favor of cooperative arms limitations. But I believe we have given them little incentive to do so. . . . We must convince them that their ambitious strategic goals must be lowered because the cost of pursuing them is too high and the chance of success too low."

A certain toughness and demonstrated willingness to unleash American technology in the face of the threatening Soviet arms buildup is sometimes necessary. But it is easy to overdo. To some outsiders, Reagan's hardline rhetoric sounds like a formula for sidetracking effective arms negotiations or at least leaving them in suspended animation for a year or two, or maybe more. Early in the campaign, close Reagan associates were quite comfortable conceding that it would be a year or two until meaningful arms negotiations began. The closer they got to Election Day, the shorter their time frame became.

To ease voters' concerns, foreign policy aides like Richard Allen drew a distinction between formal negotiations and "talks" with the Russians. Talks, Allen contended, could start very early and deal not only with the arms race but such other crucial topics as avoiding accidental conflicts around the world. Moreover, the Reagan high command envisages fairly regular high-level — though not summit — meetings with the Russians and plans to upgrade the importance and functions of the American Ambassador in Moscow as a channel for communicating with the Politburo.

Nonetheless, Reagan himself seems to feel that it will take time for the Soviets to adjust to his view of the world and his way of doing business. They will choose to be more flexible, he contends, only when confronted with the hard reality of renewed American determination and military readiness to protect vital interests and allies abroad. And for all his pre-election protestations about not wanting a showdown, there is a hint that he believes that it will take some test of strength to alter Soviet calculations.

VIII

The Final Campaign

Adam Clymer

Ronald Reagan exited stage right in 1976, hailing the very conservative party platform that had been conceded to his supporters by President Gerald Ford's forces as a "banner of bold unmistakeable colors with no pale pastel shades." His next entrance was clearly a move to the middle, if not in substance, then certainly in tone. By the time he announced his candidacy for the Republican presidential nomination formally on November 13, 1979, he was courting party moderates, putting up with some criticism from his own right, and looking forward, perhaps a bit too soon, to the general election. Explaining his candidate's rather bland announcement speech that night, Reagan's press secretary, James Lake, offered the candid explanation, "You use angry words, maybe, to get nominated, but not to get elected."

Reagan's path from the Kansas City Convention Center in August 1976 to the grand ballroom of the Waldorf-Astoria in New York City in 1979 was rather simple, and rather obvious. After a light schedule of campaigning in the fall of 1976, one which was aimed more at helping conservative Republicans and extolling the platform's virtues than at allout assistance for Ford, Reagan went back to writing a syndicated newspaper column, making radio commentaries, and speaking at conventions and Republican Party functions. "He was doing the very thing one would do if one were running full-time, having his options open. Nothing was certain, but he was very robust and physically young for his age," said his friend, William French Smith, a Los Angeles attorney who has been part of Reagan's inner circle since Reagan first got into politics.

But there was one special step he took, creating a political action committee out of leftover 1976 campaign funds (money that came in too late to be used that year and that Reagan could legally have pocketed and paid taxes on). He put about $1 million into the organization, run out of a small office in Santa Monica, California, which helped Republican candidates, mostly conservatives, and put out a sharp-tongued newsletter that kept Reagan in touch with his faithful supporters. It was named *Citizens for the Republic,* using the initials CFTR after an initial choice of CFR outraged some on the right because it reminded them of the dreaded Council on Foreign Relations.

In 1977 he sounded off against the Panama Canal treaties, going on national television to oppose them, but it was not a full-time preoccupation. They were ratified the next year anyway, though in the process Reagan's closest friend in elective politics, Senator Paul Laxalt of Nevada, developed a reputation in Washington for leading the opposition to the pacts with dignity and without demagoguery, a reputation that enhanced his ability to sell the Reagan candidacy among his colleagues.

In 1978 he campaigned hard for Republicans, even such moderates as Senator Charles H. Percy of Illinois. But talk that he was moderating his views and concern about his age — he would be sixty-nine less than three weeks before the 1980 New Hampshire primary — served as an excuse for one challenge, the candidacy of Representative Philip M. Crane, a handsome, very conservative Illinois Republican who said on August 2, 1978, that he was running but promised to drop out if it ever seemed to him he was endangering a true conservative's chance of winning the nomination. (In fact, Crane's scattering of support in the 1980 Iowa caucuses may have been enough to deny Reagan victory there, but Crane did not drop out until Reagan's nomination was all but certain two months later.)

In 1979 Reagan first set up an exploratory committee, one of those political fictions that lets money be raised and spent without subjecting the would-be candidate to real scrutiny. In Reagan's case, it also permitted his radio broadcasts to continue without hindrance from the equal-time rule. Reagan held back from saying very much that was new or exciting, telling an interviewer "you have to ration your ammunition." He kept up his schedule of speeches around the country, combining those banquet affairs with political meetings and attracting local headlines with his bluntly phrased views, such as the comment, after the murder of the United States ambassador to Afghanistan, that "I'm beginning to wonder if the symbol of the United States pretty soon isn't going to be an ambassador with a flag under his arm climbing into the escape helicopter."

If he made one significant speech before November 13, it was a San Diego address in September rejecting the new Strategic Arms Limitation Treaty, a speech in which he argued that the treaty was flawed because it did not provide for reduction in arms, and did not secure the United States adequately. Its bottom-line opposition was what his conservative constituency demanded. But the tone was calm and reasoned. There was no ideological raw meat in it.

Most of the 1976 campaign team was back for 1980, talking confidently to reporters about how this time they would really have time to plan a campaign right. John P. Sears was traveling the country, preaching Reagan's virtues to the nonbelievers, moderate Governors such as William G. Milliken in Michigan or James A. Rhodes in Ohio. Old supporters had been signed up again, pros such as Gerald Carmen in New Hampshire, and some new friends had been found. The most prominent of them was Drew Lewis, the former Pennsylvania state Republican chairman who had held the line for Ford there in 1976 after the Schweiker gambit, but signed on with Reagan in early 1979.

But the 1979 Reagan campaign looked better from afar than at close range. Despite constant promises, nothing much was happening on developing the detailed positions on issues that everyone agreed Reagan needed. The SALT speech was an exception to that pattern, with a lot of effort going into briefing Reagan before the speech was written. Geographically, the campaign was split between the east and west coasts, with Sears dividing his time between Los Angeles and Washington, where Charles Black headed up the field operation. And, with Sears in charge, frictions developed that led first to the departure of Lyn Nofziger, Reagan's longtime press aide who was unaccountably put in charge of fund raising, and then of Mike Deaver, another old hand who crossed Sears. David Keene, who worked the Southern states in 1976, never joined the 1980 effort, choosing instead to serve as political director for George Bush, a position better than he could have had with the Reagan campaign.

Still, the campaign suffered no significant setbacks in 1979. Other candidates sought to win headlines and respectability with victories, or even second-place finishes, in straw polls conducted at party dinners, mostly in Iowa. They were looking for shortcuts, thinking that a straw poll in Ames in October 1975 had been the key to Jimmy Carter's rise to prominence. George Bush won a few in Iowa, where he was making an intense effort. He won one at a Maine Republican convention on November 3 and used a *New York Times* headline on it to raise several hundred thousand dollars. The real loser in that contest was Senator Howard H. Baker, Jr., of Tennessee, who had scheduled his announcement and first two days of campaigning to wind up with a victory in Portland. Reagan did better two weeks later, taking his opening tour to Kissimmee, Florida, just across the road from Disney World, and spoiling John B. Connally's hopes for a headline from a Florida state Republican convention by winning handily. Connally finished third, behind Bush, after spending more than $300,000 on a contest in which no delegates were at stake.

But the Reagan campaign was trying too hard to stay above the battle. The campaign recalled, in its self-confidence, those early 1972 bumper stickers that said, "President Muskie. Don't You Feel Better Already?" That attitude showed when he declined an invitation to join other Republican candidates in Des Moines on January 5, 1980, sixteen days before Iowa Republicans, in precinct meetings, would begin the actual process of picking delegates to the nominating convention in Detroit in July. The others all turned up: Bush, Baker, Crane, Connally, Senator Bob Dole of Kansas, and Representative John B. Anderson of Illinois. Opinions differed about who actually won the debate, but it was clear in the immediate reactions of Iowa Republicans, and then from a poll by the *Des Moines Register*, that Reagan had lost by his absence.

Ducking that debate, on the grounds that it would be divisive, was not the only reflection of a take-it-for-granted approach. Reagan campaigned much less than his rivals did. Despite the conservatism of Iowa Republicanism, and the fact that his own days as a sports broadcaster in Davenport and Des Moines left fond memories of "Dutch" Reagan, as he was known in the thirties, he lost to Bush in those caucuses on January 21. Or at least he probably lost. Computer failures and fatigue left the results incomplete, with Bush narrowly ahead, when the Iowa Republican Party quit counting.

There was a ragged air to the Reagan campaign in those days. In a television interview broadcast January 27, he suggested blockading Cuba in retaliation for the Soviet invasion of Afghanistan. In Jacksonville, Florida, three days later, he said that while he thought the spread of nuclear weapons to Pakistan was regrettable, "I just don't think it's any of our business." Aides tried to get him to modify the position and arranged a special briefing for reporters, but Reagan stuck to his guns. A few days later he told a Polish-Italian joke to reporters. One of them had invited him to tell the story, but the reaction was hostile anyway.

But there was also one key change of strategy. Reagan decided to debate other candidates. He agreed to two debates in New

Hampshire and one in South Carolina. That decision was probably necessary to his eventual nomination, but he was also greatly assisted by the mistakes of his new rival. The Bush campaign was not taking advantage of the former C.I.A. chief's surprise victory in Iowa. Polls did show Bush pulling ahead of Reagan in the opinion of Republicans, but they rarely showed much in the way of commitment from the Bush supporters. Bush did not use his month of prominence, the period between the Iowa caucuses and the New Hampshire primary, to give them any reasons why they should be for him, except that he had the "Big Mo" or momentum from Iowa and was "Up for the Eighties." He jogged almost daily, and indeed looked more vigorous than Reagan. But as long as Reagan was not doddering, that was not enough. Reagan put in hard campaign days of his own and celebrated his birthday with a public flourish.

Debates in political campaigns have a way of freezing the action. Their anticipation matters more than the controversies that precede them, such as Reagan's comments on Cuba, or his assertions that there was more oil in Alaska than almost anywhere. He was, in fact, gaining some ground with serious campaigning before the first of the New Hampshire debates took place on February 20 in Manchester, featuring the Iowa cast, plus Reagan. He made a strong impression, defending Republican concern with "single issues" such as gun control and abortion as an "expression of a discontent on the part of the people, a feeling that the old traditional values upon which our civilization is built are fading away." Later polling suggested strongly that Reagan had won, but at the time most newspaper and television reporters thought no one had come out that clearly ahead or behind.

There was no such uncertainty about the second one, on February 23 in Nashua. Reagan and Sears changed the political landscape and made a fool out of Bush. Reagan had agreed to debate Bush, plainly his main rival by then, alone in Nashua just three days before the first primary on the mainland (Bush had prevailed a few days earlier in Puerto Rico, but nobody cared). The other five candidates complained bitterly, saying they were being unfairly excluded from a critical event in a critical state.

The New Hampshire primary is an odd institution, taking place in a state dominated by an intensely right-wing newspaper, *The Manchester Union-Leader*, and one which has a remarkable dissimilarity to the nation as a whole, since it is populated almost entirely by whites and lacks a single big city. Still, not since the primary was initiated in 1952 has anyone been elected President without having won in New Hampshire (though some have been nominated and then lost the general election). The event gets vast television coverage that sets the tone for much of the campaign to follow. It has an impact far beyond the twenty-two Republican delegates it elects, or 1.1 percent of those who would participate at the convention in Detroit.

The other candidates succeeded in getting the Federal Election Commission to decide that holding the debate would amount to an illegal campaign contribution if the *Nashua Telegraph* went ahead with it as planned. So Reagan agreed to pay $3,500 to rent the high school where it was held, and Sears made sure the other candidates would be available. Then Reagan invited them to join in. Everybody came to Nashua wondering what was going to happen, and candidates, campaign managers, and hundreds of reporters milled around the high school in confusion. The newspaper insisted on keeping the other candidates out, and Bush said he was obliged to stick to his commitment to the paper, whose management was close to Hugh Gregg, a former Governor and Bush's campaign manager.

So Reagan marched into the hall with four other candidates in tow. Connally was away campaigning in South Carolina. The *Telegraph's* editor insisted the others could not speak, and tried to cut off Reagan's microphone when he began to explain the situation to the confused audience. In one of those moments of politically perfect exasperation (such as the "There you go, again" putdown of President Carter eight months later in their only debate in Cleveland), Reagan pushed on and declared, "I paid for the microphone, Mr. Green." He then told the audience he wanted the others in, but the newspaper did not want them, and he had decided to go ahead because the audience was waiting. That done, the others left to hold a joint press conference in which they attacked Bush for presumption and said he was dividing the party. Dole said they had been treated like "second class citizens." Baker contended Bush's actions "diminished our chances" to beat the Democrats.

It hardly mattered that Reagan easily bested the flustered Bush in the debate itself. He came across as forceful, decisive, and concerned about others. Bush came across as stiff and legalistic. And it mattered not at all that the editor's name was Breen, not Green.

February 26 was a crucial day in the Reagan campaign, but not just because of the primary. In the late afternoon Sears was fired, and Black and Lake went with him. Reagan was persuaded that Sears was not managing the campaign, whatever his talents as a strategist. Laxalt and Edwin Meese, III, his chief of staff while Governor of California, were the key movers in this coup, a successful counterattack to a move to get rid of Meese. The public explanation leaned heavily on the dangerous pace at which the campaign had been spending money, a serious problem because of the $18 million Federal spending limit. But there was plainly an undertone of opposition to Sears both from old retainers of Reagan and from conservatives who still resented the Schweiker move in 1976. Many of them said proudly the next day that without Sears around it would now be easier to count on conservative support.

A few hours later it was clear that Reagan had won a landslide victory in New Hampshire, that Bush's soft support had evaporated in the last few days. A *New York Times*/CBS News Poll made it clear that the Nashua events greatly accelerated Reagan's gains. The Californian got 50 percent of the votes, Bush only 23 percent.

Several months later, the ousted Lake would observe that after New Hampshire Reagan won the nomination "on automatic pilot." It worked out pretty much that way in the end, but there was some turbulence along the way. First, it was not clear whether the new campaign team, headed by William J. Casey, a New York Republican of Reagan's age, and by Meese, had the skills of Sears and Black, especially the ability to respond to suddenly developing problems.

The Sunday morning after the New Hampshire primary it looked as if they might have to. Former President Gerald R. Ford gave an interview to *The New York Times* in which he invited the Republican Party to ask him to get into the race. Ford said he had been privately urged by several party leaders to get in, though he would not name them. (In late October he said Governor Rhodes of Ohio had been one of them.) He said Reagan could not win the general election because he was "perceived as a most conservative Republican."

"A very conservative Republican," he said in the interview in his home in Rancho Mirage, California, "can't win in a national election."

While Reagan gamely said he would welcome Ford into the race, his staff was worried. It was very late to try, because many filing dates for primaries that elected delegates to the Republican National Convention had already passed. But they worried that Ford could put support and money together in a hurry and outspend them by a wide margin, even winning California's winner-take-all primary.

There was nothing they could do but sit and wait. Ford consulted everywhere he went, but found that the support he hoped to hear was inaudible. Rhodes, greatly impressed when Reagan crushed Connally in the South Carolina primary March 8, then urged the former President not to make himself look silly by a foolish quest. On March 15, after a tearful meeting at Rancho Mirage, Ford announced he would not run.

The rest of the primary campaign was basically uneventful. Bush beat Reagan in Pennsylvania, came surprisingly close in Texas, and then beat him in Michigan in May. But the night of the

Michigan primary, to Bush's dismay, the television networks announced that Reagan already had enough delegates to be nominated.

Still, even if he was winning, and occasionally attracting the votes of blue-collar workers and nominal Democrats in states like Illinois and Wisconsin, he was rarely exceeding 50 percent of the vote. Reagan was winning, comfortably enough to have no real worry about getting nominated. But he was reaching out in only a limited way. In particular, he was not winning votes in the traditional Republican suburbs. Bush, who was much more like the inhabitants of Bucks County, Pennsylvania, or Birmingham, Michigan, than Reagan, was getting their votes.

But Reagan was winning, with an approach that said the nation's most troubling problems — inflation, energy, the hostages in Iran, even the weakening of family ties — could be solved, relatively easily. About the only consistent specific was his call for 10 percent Federal income tax cuts in each of the next three years. Generally, his prescription, again and again, was for government to get out of the way. In Greensburg, Pennsylvania, on April 10, he talked about energy in the same way he talked about other issues, and asked rhetorically, "Does it take a genius to figure out that the answer to our having all we need and no more being dependent on OPEC is to turn the energy industry loose to produce all the natural oil and the natural gas that is to be found here?" Inflation, he had insisted in Amarillo, Texas, the day before, and repeated wherever he went, was caused by government spending. "Government causes inflation. We've got to make the government make it go away."

Although there were decisions to be made about how to expand the staff, and plans to start making for the fall, by the time June 3 came, signaling the end of the primaries, there was only one important decision to be made that had a deadline on it — the choice of a vice-presidential candidate. Again, as in 1976, Reagan approached it with little obeisance to tradition. In 1976, the Schweiker ploy had been a gamble of necessity. In 1980, the Ford opening always had a perfectly safe fallback position in the eventual choice of Bush.

It was a bold idea, to be sure, to get a former President to agree to run for Vice-President, especially after he had considered running against Reagan for the nomination himself. Reagan plainly believed that Ford would give him the best chance of winning, a view his polltaker, Richard Wirthlin, and many of his other advisers shared.

To get him, Reagan tried to overcome the former President's fears about demeaning his former office with the trivialities of second place. He tried to offer Ford real power, a supervisory role at the White House over some of the functions of government. There remain some disagreements about what went on in Detroit on July 16. The basic dispute is over how much the Ford people, especially Henry A. Kissinger, the former Secretary of State, asked for and how much Reagan's negotiators offered without being asked. But none of those arguments, even if the record is ever completed, reach to what Reagan's bottom line would have been (or Ford's either).

At the least, the whole exercise displayed a remarkably naive hopefulness about deciding very deep questions regarding the heart of the Federal government on a preposterously short timetable. It had one significant side effect, that of burying Ford's doubts about Reagan and lifting his level of trust to the point where he campaigned continually for Reagan in the fall. (Ford's disdain for Carter played perhaps an even greater role in that effort, but he cheerfully disavowed his previous criticisms of Reagan as someone with a "penchant for offering simplistic solutions to hideously complex problems.") Ford's attitude about the failed efforts in Detroit, in retrospect, is that everything really worked out quite well with the eventual choice of Bush. He said of Reagan's initiative, "I don't fault him for wanting to try. I think it shows some innovativeness. He made a very good faith effort. But I guess, to try to restructure the Vice-Presidency during forty-eight hours in a convention atmosphere was just too much."

This initiative, and the Schweiker move too, are interesting and perhaps significant because they seem to reflect the approach of a politician who came to his trade rather late in life, without having been brought up to believe that there were unbreakable taboos in politics. "Certainly he has a respect for tradition," said William French Smith, "but not for tradition's sake. If there is some good reason to depart, he says, 'Well, why not?'" Or, as Sears put it, "If you came to him with a different idea, he never told you, 'Things just aren't done that way.' He asked you to explain, and if your idea was convincing, he would buy it."

The vice-presidential confusion, with messages going back and forth from the top floor to the one below in the glistening modern Detroit Plaza Hotel ("Henry Ford's bowling trophy," some Detroiters call it), and all manner of rumor on the convention floor Wednesday night, at least brought the thirty-second Republican National Convention to life. There was Ford, talking with Walter Cronkite about a "co-Presidency." Any number of lawyers, from William French Smith to Ford's own ally, John O. Marsh, were dealing with the constitutional issue of running mates resident in the same state. Some Reagan aides, like Nofziger (who had returned as press secretary), were afraid that Meese and Wirthlin were being tricked by Kissinger. Bush waited gamely at another hotel, the Pontchartrain, and then, to his surprise, got the word. Laxalt, who wanted Ford but considered himself a good second choice, exploded when told the decision had been made for Bush and didn't bother to listen to Reagan's acceptance address the next night. *The Chicago Sun-Times'* headline, proclaiming the Ford decision to accept became a collectors' item. *The New York Times* simply held its second edition press run until things became clear, as they did when Reagan brought Bush to the hall, introduced him as his running choice, and attested to his belief in the platform.

Otherwise, the convention had some right-wing self-indulgence with a platform that dropped forty years of more or less consistent support of the Equal Rights Amendment and favored a constitutional amendment prohibiting abortions, along with Federal judges who were against them. It called for repeal of the 55-mile-per-hour speed limit, and hailed the private automobile as a vital symbol of "personal mobility and freedom." But at the same time its economic policy was decidedly more progressive, more concerned with unemployment in particular, than most such documents.

Reagan's acceptance address, capably delivered, had almost no lines in it that were faintly memorable. He began with a pledge of support for equal rights for women (but not the amendment) and ended up quoting Franklin Delano Roosevelt (on reducing the size of the Federal government). It was good politics, and good television, but it was still the Wednesday night circus that recalled H.L. Mencken, writing in 1924: "There is something about a national convention that makes it as fascinating as a revival or a hanging. It is vulgar, it is ugly, it is stupid, it is tedious, it's hard upon both the cerebral centers and the gluteus maximus, and yet it is somehow charming. One sits through long sessions wishing heartily that all the delegates were dead and in hell and then suddenly there comes a show so gaudy and hilarious, so melodramatic and obscene, so unimaginably exhilarating and preposterous that one lives a gorgeous year in an hour."

It is easy to exaggerate the importance of anyone's strategy in assessing the outcome of the 1980 presidential election. It was not decided by Carter's campaign mistakes or by Reagan's brilliance, much less that of their ad men, pollsters, and other advisers, no matter how important those worthies think themselves.

The simple fact is the nation had an unpopular Democratic President, whose accomplishments lay in areas where no votes were to be found (the Panama Canal Treaties, or even the Camp David Agreement) and whose failures, especially unemployment, most hurt the Northern, big-city voters without whom no Democrat can expect to win. He never found a way to concede failures in his first term, and while he groped for ways to convey a vision for the future, it always sounded more like a blueprint than a vision. He had come through a bitter fight for his nomination without ever conceding enough to the losers to win their allegiance. They came back, by and large, but to beat Reagan, not to win for Carter. He had the odd feature of John B. Anderson's independent candidacy to contend with, too, and it appeared that Anderson drew more support from potential Carter voters than from those who might have been Reagan's. The Republicans were better organized than the Democrats in much of the country, and took advantage of the quirks of the Federal election law to spend more money. Most of all, the electoral vote charts made it clear all along that Carter had to win more of the close states with big chunks of electoral votes than did Reagan.

The Reagan strategy really required a steady, calm approach in which, despite all the criticisms that were heard about the folly of "sitting on a lead," it made sense to do pretty much just that, even when the lead looked very narrow in terms of national polls. It was a very slow-moving campaign, in which both vote percentages and perceptions of candidates hardly changed from Labor Day to late October. The public seemed anything but delighted with its choice of candidates. But Reagan ("the ultimate, laid-back Californian," as David Keene once called him) had the personality to stick with unexciting advice and win with it.

The first element of that approach involved not saying anything stupid, not giving the Carter side a chance to label the challenger as too dumb or too ignorant for the job he sought. Reagan, whose 1976 campaign was dotted with observations better left unsaid, had avoided this problem pretty well in 1980. There was a period in April when he couldn't seem to get facts straight on such matters as the GI Bill of Rights, but it all seemed rather trivial.

In August, however, Reagan kept saying awkward things. As Bush was dispatched to China in a move to show the Chinese that they could live with conservative Republicans who had opposed the terms on which full diplomatic relations were established by Carter in 1978, Reagan began emphasizing how highly he regarded Taiwan and talked of reestablishing "official" relations with that island. Then, attending a born-again Christians' convention in Dallas, Reagan said at a press conference that legitimate doubts had been raised about the Darwinian theory of evolution, and he believed competing theories should be taught in the schools, too. And in Chicago he told the Veterans of Foreign Wars that the war in Vietnam was a "noble cause." Reagan seemed willing, in short, to chase after porcupines and revive old causes, issues of 1924, 1952, and 1968 on which no one was going to vote in 1980, unless they voted against a sixty-nine-year-old candidate who seemed fascinated with old issues.

Perhaps even more important than any direct negative reaction to these comments was that they were a distraction. If there was one sure way to beat Jimmy Carter, it was to keep attention focused on the economy. In August Reagan didn't do that.

But in August it may not have mattered. Traditionally, a presidential election begins in earnest on Labor Day. And on Labor Day Reagan was at his best at Liberty State Park in Jersey City, talking about the greatness of America with the Statue of Liberty and Ellis Island behind him, and assailing Carter on the economy. He did it, in particular, with one favorite line that played on criticism of his calling the situation a "depression" the week before. (He always attributed the criticism to Carter; in fact it came from his own advisers.) Reagan said, "Recession is when your neighbor loses his job. Depression is when you lose yours. And recovery is when Jimmy Carter loses his."

That was the message on the evening television news, that and a staged backyard barbecue with workers, some unemployed, in Detroit. But then at the Michigan State Fair he hit out at Carter and said of the President's appearance that day in Tuscumbia, Alabama, "He's opening his campaign in the city that gave birth to and is the parent body of the Ku Klux Klan." Carter jumped on the statement and so, spontaneously, did several Southern Governors. Reagan apologized quickly, but it still seemed to more than a few Southerners that he was willing to sacrifice their self-esteem for votes somewhere else.

But that was the last time Reagan said something that really hurt him. He did proclaim the air pollution problem under control in Ohio, and then had his airplane diverted when returning to

California because of the worst smog in years. He said a number of things that were just plain not true as the campaign went on, such as denying that he ever proposed making Social Security voluntary or that he said nuclear nonproliferation was none of the United States' business. But he never really got in trouble again, and one shrewd long-term observer of Reagan campaigns, Lou Cannon of *The Washington Post*, pointed out that in every race he had ever run, Reagan had begun badly.

The second key piece of the Reagan strategy was to deflect Carter's criticism, especially the line of attack that suggested Reagan was, as the Californian once put it, some sort of "mad bomber." This was the single most clearly telegraphed punch of the campaign, and, even so, it had an impact. In late October, a *New York Times*/CBS News Poll found 39 percent of the public answered yes when asked, "Do you think that if Ronald Reagan were elected President in 1980, he would get us into a war?"

The Reagan forces fought this theme in various ways. Their first television commercial of the fall had Reagan telling the camera, "Of all the objectives we seek, first and foremost is the establishment of world peace." Much later, he bought half an hour of national television time to talk about foreign policy and defense without seeming scary.

But probably their most effective weapon in deflecting this criticism, and another, that Reagan was a racist, was Carter himself. The President overdid the attack. Once in a while, he did it well, arguing that Reagan's history of talking about using force in one crisis after another was itself a threat to international stability. But he got more attention when he went further, as when he told a Torrance, California, audience on September 22 that by their votes "you will determine what kind of life you and your families will have, whether this nation will make progress or go backward, and whether we have peace or war." Reagan snapped back that this attack was "beneath decency."

But he did even better when Carter charged that Reagan's election could mean that "Americans might be separated, blacks from whites, Jews from Christians, North from South, rural from urban." It wasn't a tough part for a skilled movie actor, and Reagan made the most of it when he replied, on all networks, "I can't be angry. I'm saddened that anyone, particularly someone who has held that position, could intimate such a thing, and I'm not asking for an apology from him. I know who I have to account to for my actions. But I think he owes the country an apology."

Reagan has a manner that contradicts the simple text of many of the things he says. He doesn't look like a mad bomber. Ultimately, the best device the Reagan forces had for countering the warmonger attack was Reagan's own manner in the October 28 debate. The percentage of Americans who said they feared war if he was elected dropped from 39 before the debate to 31 percent afterward.

A third element was to simply not panic. National polls showed the race very close, and occasionally even put Carter ahead. Inside the Reagan camp it was important to remember that the election was not one national vote, but fifty-one separate elections choosing 538 electors. Their calculations of that electoral vote never showed them behind. By and large they remembered and did not react hastily.

What they feared most was an "October surprise" in foreign policy, most of all the return of the hostages from Iran, an issue that had served Carter well in the primaries. When something seemed to be happening in mid-October, Reagan attacked Carter for tolerating the continuing captivity, while other Republicans laid a covering fire of accusations suggesting Carter was manipulating the issue to win votes. Reagan generally took the high road, proclaiming at the Alfred E. Smith Dinner in New York that, whatever the political impact, "no one in America will rejoice more than I" at their return. He consistently responded cautiously. When an agreement on return appeared imminent on the last day of the campaign, he prepared but did not use language for a national television speech that dealt with the issue. Instead, he stuck largely to the economy.

But not panicking does not mean never changing what you're doing. For several weeks, it seemed that the Reagan campaign thought it did. Then, in one week in mid-October, Reagan came out with a promise to put a woman on the Supreme Court and with the decision to debate Carter. Earlier, he had wanted a three-way debate, including Anderson, for the same reason that Carter had opposed one. His staff figured that Anderson would hurt Carter most. When Reagan and Anderson debated in Baltimore on September 21, Reagan profited most, not from any particular specific argument he made, but from his inspirational closing argument: "Some people in high positions of leadership tell us that the answer is to retreat, that the best is over. For 200 years we've lived in the future, believing that tomorrow would be better than today and today would be better than yesterday. I still believe that. I'm not running for the Presidency because I believe I can solve the problems we've discussed tonight. I believe the people of this country can."

But the gains he made in terms of public impressions of him, on questions like whether he understood the complicated problems of the White House, had largely worn off by late October. The agreement to accept a revised invitation from the League of Women Voters, at the very moment when Carter's advisers were trying to devise a way to get out of their long-standing demand for a one-on-one debate, was a matter of considerable argument within the Reagan camp. Some saw no reason to take a chance. Others, including Reagan in particular, thought there was no reason to fear a debate with Carter.

All year long, the Carter forces had licked their chops in anticipation of getting the President, with his command of detail, in a debate with Reagan. They were sure he would seem more presidential and Reagan would seem foolish. No matter that George Bush and Howard Baker had thought the same. The night of the confrontation in Cleveland, however, Carter had more details, and more accuracy for that matter, but it was Reagan's manner that was plainly most effective. He sounded reasonable and in control. Carter sounded anxious, pressing.

It was hardly a brilliant exposition of national policy. Carter's citation of daughter Amy as authority for the importance of nuclear weaponry as a campaign issue, and his metaphor of a continent-wide railroad train with fifty tons of TNT in each car for a fifty megaton nuclear bomb was no less inspiring than Reagan's metaphor for joblessness: "If all the unemployed today were in a single line, allowing two feet for each one of them, that line would reach from New York City to Los Angeles, California."

But debating points seem to matter less than impressions of personalities in such debates. As in 1960 and 1976, the challenger established himself in a debate with either the incumbent President or Vice-President.

Besides his style, Reagan did finally manage, after eight weeks of more failures than successes, to make the economy the issue. It wasn't that inflation and unemployment were not affecting choices of presidential candidates. It is clear that they were, all along, with Carter losing plenty of Democratic and Independent voters who thought they were worse off financially than a year earlier. But the other issues, the ones that helped Reagan and the ones that hurt him, had rarely permitted economic questions to lead the evening television news two days in a row. In the debate, Reagan fixed that. Talking of the decision to be made on Election Day, he said: "I think when you make that decision it might be well if you could ask yourself, are you better off than you were four years ago? Is it easier for you to go and buy things in the stores than it was four years ago? Is there more or less unemployment in the country than there was four years ago?"

Reagan's solutions, which Carter said were "completely irresponsible and would result in inflationary pressures which would destroy this nation," did not matter. He had invited the nation to conduct a referendum on Jimmy Carter. One week later, the nation took him up on it, and in a landslide Ronald Wilson Reagan was elected the fortieth President of the United States.

IX

Mr. Reagan Goes to Washington

Hedrick Smith

On Election Day, Ronald and Nancy Reagan, he in a checkered red shirt and she in red-plaid shirt and slacks, voted on paper ballots in a neighbor's home. Their precinct in Pacific Palisades is such a small and exclusive residential enclave that there are no public buildings to serve as polling places. Lawrence Welk, the band leader, voted a bit ahead of the Reagans, but Sylvester Stallone, the movie actor and director, had not shown up by the time they left.

A bit later, Reagan had a haircut, shine, and manicure at Drucker's Barber Shop in Beverly Hills and lunched on tuna salad, iced tea, and ice milk with Ed Meese and Mike Deaver, two of his closest political aides. Whenever either one began to talk of victory or transition planning, the candidate knocked on wood or refused to join in, not wanting to jinx his chances.

In mid-afternoon his pollster, Richard Wirthlin, dropped by Reagan's house to give him advance word of the electoral landslide that was in the making. Shortly after 5:30 P.M., Pacific time, fairly soon after the East Coast polls had begun to close, Reagan was in the shower when Jimmy Carter called. Deaver went to get him. Reagan stepped out of the shower and wrapped a towel around himself as he took the phone to accept the personal concession and congratulations of the thirty-ninth President of the United States.

There, in that stark instant, this son of a shoe salesman from Tampico, Illinois, this former actor whose greatest ambition in his youth had been to become a play-by-play announcer for the Chicago Cubs, was transformed into the most powerful political figure in the world. This was the climax of an unorthodox political odyssey that began fifteen years earlier, when, at the age of fifty-four, Reagan was persuaded by his California business friends to enter the political arena and run for Governor. Three times he tried for the Presidency, and twice he failed. Now, at the age of sixty-nine, he had become the oldest man in American history to stand at the threshold of that awesome office.

His electoral campaign was a stunning success. He had stolen Jimmy Carter's Southern base, smashed the incumbent's expected strength in the East, and taken command of the battleground states of the Middle West. The entire West had gone for him, as expected, to complete the rout. More than that, on Reagan's coattails and on the tide of an overwhelming vote of protest against Carter and the Democrats, the Republican Party had sailed into control of the Senate for the first time in twenty-six years, gaining twelve new Senate seats plus thirty-three in the House of Representatives. Although the Democrats still had control of the House, Reagan could anticipate a conservative philosophical majority in that chamber. In one day, the political map of America had been redrawn, and Reagan now dominated the national landscape.

That night, at the victory celebration in the glittering ballroom of the Century Plaza Hotel in Los Angeles, the ebullient, smiling, handsome new President-elect took his bows and shared some thoughts about the Presidency.

"Do you know," he told his delirious partisans, "Abe Lincoln, the day after his election to the Presidency, gathered in his office the newsmen who had been covering his campaign and he said to them: 'Well, boys, your troubles are over now; mine have just begun.' I think I know what he meant. Lincoln may have been concerned in the troubled times in which he became President. But I don't think he was afraid. And I am not frightened by what lies ahead and I don't believe the American people are frightened by what lies ahead. Together, we're going to do what has to be done. We're going to put America back to work again."

It was risky of Reagan to invite such exalted comparisons and to set up such high expectations. For those with an ear for American political history heard not only the voice of Lincoln but also a subliminal echo of Franklin Delano Roosevelt, Reagan's early hero, telling a generation of downhearted Americans half a century ago to take courage for, "We have nothing to fear but fear itself," and of John F. Kennedy, in his high, choppy Boston accent, declaring in 1960 that it was high time to "get America moving again."

Campaigning for the Presidency, Reagan often evoked FDR, asking, in effect, to be seen as the leader of a new political revolution, the father of a conservative renaissance that will radically alter the American concept of governing as Roosevelt did with the New Deal. Repeatedly, Reagan had made the point that it is he who kept the true faith with the original Roosevelt, who campaigned in 1932 on the promise that government "costs too much" and that "we must abolish useless offices," while the Roosevelt who took office changed course and launched an era of governmental growth and activism that Reagan has spent the latter half of his lifetime opposing.

Reagan's supporters relish the notion that he could become a conservative Republican version of Roosevelt. "I divide American Presidents into journeymen Presidents who run the machine and make it go, and symbolic Presidents who make radical changes," says Senator Howard Baker of Tennessee, the new Republican Majority Leader. "Ford and Carter, and even Truman and Johnson, were journeymen Presidents. Roosevelt and Nixon were symbolic Presidents. Nixon made drastic changes in foreign policy. He was trying to rearrange the world, alter the status quo. Roosevelt made fundamental changes in domestic affairs until World War II came along. I think Reagan will be a symbolic President. I do think he'll make a sustained drive to change the size and cost of government. I do think he'll try to change the system of delivering government services and sending Federal aid and categorical grants to localities. His tax policy is fundamentally different. And what also marks him as different is his ability to go to the people and mobilize public support. Nixon didn't have that, but Roosevelt did."

Some presidential scholars, such as James David Barber of Duke University, discount Reagan's upbeat speechifying as simplistic and unrealistic cheerleading without solid purpose and vision. They expect him to be a fairly passive President, a throwback to the conservative, pro-business quietism of Warren G. Harding or William Howard Taft. "He's a 'Music Man' who goes around encouraging people and who wants the affection of the public," says Barber. "His danger is that he's so open to political sharks." However, other scholars, such as Tom Cronin of Colorado College, sense a whiff of the Kennedy magic and glamour in Reagan's rhetoric and his political presence.

"John F. Kennedy had a way with words, a way of talking about issues in simple terms that made them interesting and got people to listen," says Cronin. "Reagan has that knack, too. And, like Kennedy, there is a contagious optimism about him. In the presidential debates, Kennedy and Reagan didn't really win on substance, but on appearance. People liked Kennedy, and I have a hunch they'll like Reagan. He realizes there's a morale problem in this country and he addresses it. The country can be quite taken by a guy who can give a fireside speech with a can-do spirit."

Of course, no stereotype fits. Reagan is a composite of some of his predecessors and something entirely new. He is closest of all to Dwight Eisenhower in tone, style, and perhaps even outlook, for both have brought to the Presidency the uncomplicated outlook of Small-Town America, an unbounded faith in free enterprise, supreme confidence in the judgment of businessmen, and the citizen politician's disdain for the excesses of government.

Like the heroic general, Reagan likes to set out the broad philosophical lines of his administration and to operate in the highly structured corporate style of a board chairman or a supreme commander making major decisions in the company of a small group of close advisers, entrusting substantial power to key Cabinet officers and aides and generally keeping himself above the political fray of the moment.

Nothing illustrates more convincingly Reagan's willingness, indeed his preference, for delegating executive authority to subordinates than his entering into negotiations with former President Ford at the Republican Convention last July for some kind of "super Vice-Presidency" as an inducement to get Ford to join the Reagan ticket. Ford's concept was that Reagan, as President, would be the chief executive officer of the government, the final authority who makes all the decisions, and that Ford, as Vice-President, would be the chief operating officer of the administration, implementing presidential decisions, supervising the White House staff, and making government work.

In principle, the idea appealed to Reagan's concept of executive organization as well as to his pragmatic political desire to have the strongest possible running mate. He showed common sense when he balked at suggestions for shared powers that threatened to dismantle his Presidency before it was won. But the whole concept harked back to Eisenhower's method of parceling out important powers to principal advisers such as Sherman Adams, his chief of staff, and Secretary of State John Foster Dulles, who often acted as his deputies with presidential authority.

Although no stepping-stone is an adequate test for the White House, Reagan seems as comfortable as Eisenhower with the fundamental, personal responsibility of the Presidency. He has never appeared to strain himself, as Carter often did, but knowing himself, he projects an easy, natural, inner confidence in his own capacity for leadership. His roots, like Ike's, are in the American heartland, the farm country of the Middle West, and those roots are never very far from the surface. For all his Hollywood background and his coterie of millionnaire California friends, Reagan, like Eisenhower, has the simple tastes, gee-whiz grin, and open charm of the boy next door.

On camera or on the stump, Reagan can be magical in his appeal. He projects as a highly moral, honest, sincere, and purposeful citizen-politician. He exudes an air of simple virtue. His aw-shucks manner and charming good looks disarm those who from a distance have thought of him as a far-right fanatic. He comes across as patently unmalicious, whatever he says. Face-to-face with the the public, his ability to reduce problems to simple propositions has common sense appeal. In that, he is like Eisenhower, even occasionally with Eisenhower's scrambled syntax.

Politically, Reagan is straightforward, uncomplicated, and even naive, though, as with Ike, there can be guile behind his seemingly artless ways. Just as often, his open candor and his naiveté have gotten him into hot water. For example, his loose-lipped directness on Vietnam and Taiwan gave him trouble during the campaign, and he suffered political embarrassment by having his negotiations with Gerald Ford rise and fall so dramatically and publicly when a more calculating politician would have kept that drama hidden behind the scenes.

Reagan's success, however, derives not from a great mastery of political maneuvering and coalition-building through long links to the fraternity of professional politicians. Like Eisenhower, he has sound, quick political instincts; the appeal of political amateurism and sincerity; and the ability to communicate over the heads of other politicians to the people.

Initially, Reagan's advisers intend him to set a fast pace in the White House, in part perhaps to counteract the Eisenhower stereotype. But temperamentally, Reagan seems far more inclined to the modest pace of the Eisenhower Presidency than the throbbing programmatic activism of FDR or Lyndon Johnson.

Eager to offset public worries about his age, Reagan campaigned long and hard from Labor Day to Election Day. As Governor of California, he occasionally worked late with the Legislature, but his natural rhythm was the 9:00-to-5:00 day with lights out around 11:00 P.M. — though the modern Presidency rarely accommodates so light a schedule. Over time, Reagan paces himself carefully and makes most decisions quickly, without agonizing unduly over them. Unlike Carter, he leaves the details to others and takes time to relax.

His style fits his outlook. Philosophically, Reagan's view of government turns on the libertarian axiom that the best government is the one that governs least. One of the lines he delivered most fervently and with greatest effect during the campaign was the persistent pledge to "get government off the people's backs." Unabashedly, he says he admires not only Eisenhower but "Silent Cal" Coolidge whose characteristically plainspoken motto for the 1920s was: "The business of America is business."

"Many people have the erroneous impression that those two spent more time golfing and relaxing than being President," Reagan remarked to an interviewer last summer. "They forget to look at the record of those years — prosperity, peace, and no inflation. Maybe I can sum it up with the words in a little plaque on my desk: 'You can accomplish much if you don't mind who gets the credit.' "

On at least two critical points, Reagan differs with Eisenhower. In the field of foreign policy, one gaping vulnerability of the former California Governor is that he lacks the long wartime experience that won Eisenhower automatic public confidence in matters of war and peace, that kept Eisenhower from entering the first Vietnam War in 1954 when some Pentagon leaders were urging it, and that left Eisenhower permanently wary of the influence of the military-industrial complex.

The other major difference is that Eisenhower was drafted into politics as a national war hero at a time when the public wanted the relief of normalcy. Reagan enters the Presidency as the spokesman for a political crusade at a time of national unease, of public cynicism, and of uncertainty about whether this nation can control its own destiny. With their friendly Dutch uncle manner, both Reagan and Eisenhower have been reassuring to the nation. But Eisenhower had no personal cause and Reagan has been leading one for nearly two decades.

His purpose is to stir the sleeping giant of America back to a sense of its manifest destiny, to oversee the restoration of an economically robust and militarily sturdy nation active in the world arena, and to rekindle the rawhide heroism and patriotic pride of John Wayne. His strategy is to roll back the Federal establishment with tax cuts, spending cuts, personnel cuts, and cutbacks in regulations that he believes will release the productive energies of free enterprise. His faith is that this nation can literally work its way out of the debilitating inflation that has it in enthrall. His instinct is to summon citizen task forces to fight the huge Federal establishment with the zesty irreverence of the Boston Tea Party. It is a tall order, many say unrealistically tall or ill-advised, but it is the vision that moves and animates Ronald Reagan.

"Many Americans today, just as they did 200 years ago, feel burdened, stifled, and sometimes even oppressed by government that has grown too large, too bureaucratic, too wasteful, too unresponsive, too uncaring about people and their problems," Reagan said on the eve of his election, in one of his most eloquent campaign speeches.

"I believe we can embark on a new age of reform in this country and an era of national renewal," he went on, "an era that will reorder the relationship between citizen and government, that will make government again responsive to people, that will revitalize the values of family, work, and neighborhood and that will restore our private and independent social institutions. These institutions always have served as both buffer and bridge between the individual and the state — and these institutions, not government, are the real sources of our economic and social progress as a people.

"That's why I've said throughout this campaign that we must control and limit the growth of Federal spending, that we must reduce tax rates to stimulate work and savings and investment. That's why I've said we can relieve labor and business of burdensome, unnecessary regulations and still maintain high standards of environmental and occupational safety.

"That's why I've said we can reduce the cost of government by eliminating billions lost to waste and fraud in the Federal bureaucracy — a problem that is now an unrelenting national scandal. And because we are a federation of sovereign states, we can restore the health and vitality of state and local governments by returning to them control over programs best run at those levels of government closer to the people. We can fight corruption while we work to bring into our government women and men of competence and high integrity."

Clearly, Reagan has his eye set on leading the Conservative Reformation, the reversal of Franklin D. Roosevelt's revolutionary New Deal, which Reagan himself once admired. Yet there is a dilemma inherent in his assertion of presidential leadership for his cause and the fierce individualism that permeates his thinking. His philosophical impulse is to foster the centrifugal forces that make national leadership so difficult today, but his political strategy requires a single-minded discipline to follow policies — especially economic policies — that has hitherto proven impossible for modern administrations and Congresses.

At the Republican Convention, Reagan touched upon a central flaw in the American system that symbolically entrusts so much responsibility to one man at the apex of power but deliberately hems him in with constitutional balances, compounded now by the fragmentation of power in Congress and the more subtle but no less palpable public distrust of authority which Reagan himself has long articulated. In accepting his party's nomination, Reagan called upon the electorate to reject Jimmy Carter's "Trust me" government that "asks that we concentrate our hopes and dreams on one man; that we trust him to do what's best for us." Reagan's own view of government, he said much more vaguely, "places trust not in one person or one party, but in those values that transcend persons and parties. The trust is where it belongs — in the people."

One fundamental test for Reagan will be how broadly or how narrowly he interprets the people's trust, how broadly or how narrowly be governs. Will he nourish the powers of the Presidency by reaching out continuously to broaden his governing coalition or

155

will he be pushed back into a New Rich narrowness that will shrink his base? Will he adjust pragmatically to political realities or break his lance on doctrinaire implementation of his pet ideas, however impolitic? Will he prove firm enough to project a clear and constant vision and yet flexible enough so that ideological rigidity does not engender stalemates that jeopardize his major objectives?

It is tempting for the Reagan entourage and its right-wing cohorts in Congress to claim an electoral mandate for a full menu of conservative measures in every field. It is also tempting for them to contend that Reagan's lopsided electoral landslide and the change of climate in Congress will enable them to roll over the Democratic opposition, presumably made pliable by the resounding defeats of prominent liberals such as Senator George McGovern of South Dakota, the 1972 presidential nominee; Senator Frank Church of Idaho, Chairman of the Senate Foreign Relations Committee; and half a dozen others. With a fifty-three to forty-seven Republican majority in the Senate, the new administration can look forward to working with such Republican conservatives as Strom Thurmond of South Carolina at the head of the Senate Judiciary Committee; Barry Goldwater of Arizona, the Intelligence Committee; Pete Domenici of New Mexico, the Budget Committee; Jesse Helms of North Carolina, the Agriculture Committee; and Jake Garn of Utah, the Banking Committee.

The liberal losses in the Senate and the addition of Republican conservatives from Alabama, Idaho, Florida, Oklahoma, and elsewhere have fueled euphoric talk about a tidal wave of conservativism which gives the new President the political clout to do pretty much as he pleases. But Reagan cannot afford the luxury of such an easy interpretation.

A closer look at the election returns reveals that his own popular vote total was 51 percent of the smallest turnout of voters in terms of percentage since 1948 — 52.4 percent of the eligible electorate. That makes Reagan the active choice of only 26.7 percent of the adult population. His popular vote percentage was the seventh lowest in twenty presidential elections in this century, and more than three out of ten who voted Republican in the presidential race told pollsters their primary motive was voting out Jimmy Carter rather than voting in Ronald Reagan.

Moreover, the Democrats still have a fifty-one-vote margin in the House and the Republican majority in the Senate is so slender that Reagan will need the Republican moderates and sometimes even party liberals in both houses to prevail on critical issues. His shrewdest political advisers have not missed noting that important Senate liberals survived in states such as California, Colorado, Vermont, Oregon, and Maryland and new Republican moderates won in Georgia, Indiana, Wisconsin, and Washington. In essence, it was more a Republican party triumph than an ideological sweep. Along with new, conservative committee chairmen in the Senate, there are several other Republicans in important spots with moderate social and political views: Charles Percy of Illinois at the Foreign Relations Committee, Mark Hatfield of Oregon at Appropriations, and Bob Dole of Kansas at Finance. Reagan can neglect these Republican moderates, not to mention the Democrats, only at his peril.

"If he can go to the people and mobilize them and reach out and broaden his coalition, then he'll do well," commented Howard Baker, the Senate Republican leader. "But if I'm wrong about him and it turns into crystalline conservatism, it won't work."

That is a point on which Reagan has had considerable tutoring. During the campaign, Reagan's advisers urged him to show compassion and moderation. He made a deliberate effort to soften dogma and reach across party lines for support. "Our message will be: We have to move ahead, but we're not going to leave anyone behind," he declared in his speech to the Republican Convention. "We Republicans believe it is essential that we maintain both the forward momentum of economic growth and the strength of the safety net beneath those in society who need help." Trying to ease fears among women and the elderly that he would neglect them, Reagan pledged to fight discrimination against women and to protect the integrity of the Social Security System.

Nonetheless, it was only natural for people to question how

much of this was political expediency in the heat of a tight campaign and how much represented lasting moderation and compassion. The real issue, however, may be less Reagan's political adaptability than the gaps in his life experience. For ironically, consistent success and the ease with which he has moved through life may have produced blind spots toward the disadvantaged that underlie some of his most fundamental political attitudes and assumptions.

Reagan has tasted some adversity, but little of his own making. He has spoken movingly of his father's drunkenness and of learning one Christmas Day during the Depression that his father had lost his job. He generally avoids mentioning that his first marriage, to film star Jane Wyman, ended in divorce, and that he is America's first divorced President. He rarely alludes to the fact that his grown children have clashed with him personally and politically and have broken away from his traditional values to pursue the very different and open lifestyles of the new generation.

Characteristically, Reagan himself has moved through life achieving success fairly easily and without suffering the sting of serious failure. Although his family beginnings were humble and he had to hunt to get his first jobs, his initial screen test got him an opening in Hollywood; and though he never became a top star, he quickly established himself as a competent leading man. His union leadership vaulted him into the world of Hollywood moguls. Over the past three decades, he has accumulated wealth and property and moved among the well-heeled corporate executives and celebrities of southern California, rarely rubbing shoulders for any period of time with less fortunate Americans.

Now there are some, including his former campaign manager, John P. Sears, who fear that the sunny existence that Reagan counts as such a blessing may prove a political handicap to him in the Presidency. Their contention is that it deprives him of true empathy for the other side of the tracks, the kind of instinctive understanding of the little people that builds credibility for a President, helps forge a durable consensus, and moderates the impulse toward rampant budget-cutting when it threatens to cause too much social pain.

Nonetheless, in terms of political tactics, Reagan has proven himself surprisingly flexible and open in spite of the dogmatic ring to his rhetoric. In 1976, when Sears went to Reagan proposing Senator Richard Schweiker of Pennsylvania as the best possible running mate to lure needed delegates from Gerald Ford, Reagan accepted without blanching at the liberalism of Schweiker's record. The tactic did not work and Reagan took great heat from unhappy conservatives, but he still reappointed Sears his 1980 campaign manager — until Sears' tactics of keeping Reagan under wraps in Iowa failed.

Again in 1980, when a new set of strategies came and told Reagan that his old rival, Gerald Ford, and his more recent rival, George Bush, had the kind of moderate images that could help him most to broaden his appeal in the general election campaign, Reagan swallowed his pride and tried first one and then the other. He passed over his personal preference, the champion of the conservatives, Senator Paul Laxalt of Nevada, a close friend and longtime conservative ally.

That same pragmatic openness has carried into the early phases of his administration, where he has resisted the pressures of the New Right for ideological purity on key appointments. On the day after the election, two prominent voices of the New Right, Paul Weyrich, head of the Committee for the Survival of a Free Congress, and Terry Dolan, Executive Director of the National Conservative Political Action Committee, warned Bush to toe the ideological line and called for the replacement of Senator Howard Baker of Tennessee, another moderate, as the prospective Republican leader of the Senate. Evidently reflecting the view of some ardent Senate conservatives, they called for Laxalt to be the new leader.

However tempting that may have sounded to Reagan, he chose shrewdly — with Laxalt's wise encouragement — to back Baker unequivocally. Within twenty-four hours, Laxalt had said he had no intention of opposing Baker, and Reagan threw his weight solidly behind the Tennesseean. At a Los Angeles press conference on November 6, Reagan scotched any conservative plans to unhorse Baker by observing that "I not only have confidence in Howard Baker but I have been informed by members of the Senate that there is no friction and there is no move going forward to change in any way . . . his position. . . . He will be the Majority Leader of the Senate."

Alerted by the bad press and costly political insulation that Jimmy Carter had built for his Presidency by initially surrounding himself with a narrow circle of fellow Georgians, Reagan passed the word in advance of the election through his longtime aide, Ed Meese, that "the senior White House staff is not going to be nine Californians." By mid-November, Reagan had quickly made good on that. He had named Meese to his top advisory position, Counselor to the President, with Cabinet rank and authority over the Domestic Council and National Security Council staffs at the White House. But for White House Chief of Staff, Reagan picked James A. Baker, III, a tall, amiable, fifty-year-old Texas lawyer who had led Ford's forces against Reagan at the 1976 Republican Convention and Bush's primary campaign against Reagan in 1980, before he joined the Reagan general election campaign in the fall as a senior adviser.

Jim Baker, a tough-minded politician with Washington experience as Under Secretary of Commerce under President Ford and a reputation for integrity and moderation, had impressed Reagan and his wife, Nancy, as he personally coached Reagan for the 1980 presidential debates and masterminded Reagan's debate strategy. Baker led the efforts to persuade Reagan to debate Carter rather than trying to coast home on a shrinking lead, and the debate paid handsome returns. Baker also scored points with Reagan's California entourage for his loyalty, his solid command of campaign finance that left them in strong shape for the final push, and his firm, decisive management of whatever fell under his tutelage. Still, the choice was unorthodox.

"Think of what that choice represents," said one Easterner who joined the campaign headquarters last summer. "It makes

Reagan the first President in years to pick a chief of staff who doesn't come from his home state or his old gang. It's a very healthy sign."

In his transition to the White House, Reagan also endorsed the decision of Meese, his transition director, to strike a balance between outspoken conservatives like William R. Van Cleave, a hawkish defense specialist from the University of California; Laurence Silberman, a San Francisco banker and former U.S. Ambassador to Yugoslavia; and former officials with less controversial reputations who gained Washington experience under the Nixon and Ford administrations.

Among them were Caspar Weinberger, former Secretary of Health, Education, and Welfare and Federal Budget Director; Anne Armstrong, former U.S. Ambassador to Great Britain; William J. Casey, former Chairman of the Securities and Exchange Commission; Gerald Parsky, a former Assistant Secretary of the Treasury; Richard Shubert, a former Under Secretary of Labor; Elizabeth Dole, a former Federal Trade Commissioner; Richard E. Wiley, former Chairman of the Federal Communications Commission; and Richard Fairbanks and Stanton Anderson, two Washington attorneys with White House experience. Overall, it was a far more experienced set of specialists than President Carter had called upon four years earlier.

The first appointments signaled Reagan's inclination to turn to talent and experience rather than to ideological allies to staff his government. Even on substance, he hinted at early flexibility. When Republicans in the lame-duck Senate began advocating quick passage of a tax cut package differing from his own pet proposals in content though not in size, Reagan responded positively. "I'd be delighted to see them do it," he said.

All this is in keeping with Reagan's record as Governor of California. He campaigned as a missionary conservative but governed, some said, as a "closet moderate." His longtime press secretary, Lyn Nofziger, once jokingly called him "a Fabian conservative."

Indeed, if Reagan's eight years as Governor of California are any guide, he will surprise many voters as a more pragmatic and moderate President than he advertised in his campaign. As Governor, he had a bumpy beginning, gradually learned the art of governance, and ultimately forged legislative compromises and accepted ideological accommodations that could hardly have been imagined during his first campaign. He promulgated huge tax increases, protected social programs, doubled the state budget, helped education, and signed a tough environmental control law and a liberalized abortion law, all at odds with his stump rhetoric. His welfare reform was a blend of his own bent for efficiency by restricting eligibility and Democratic generosity in the form of more liberal benefits for those who qualified. But philosophical inconsistencies, in the name of realism, never troubled Reagan then or since. He still feels he has a solidly conservative record, and among his most proudly proclaimed achievements was his $5.7 billion in tax rebates, mostly to local governments.

"There are some people who think you should, on principle, jump off the cliff with the flag flying if you can't get everything you want," he said, rebutting the criticism from the ideological right. "If I found when I was Governor that I could not get 100 percent of what I asked for, I took 80 percent." Often, he settled for a good deal less, or reversed direction entirely.

Reagan has the capacity, once dissuaded from a long-held view, to shift ground quickly and to extricate himself, sometimes with a touch of humor that eases the political pain.

In California, he had campaigned vigorously against a state withholding tax. On this key symbolic issue, he said, his feet were set in cement. But in 1971 the state's finances were in such dire straits that his financial advisers informed him that the only way to deal with the situation was a state withholding tax. Reagan called an emergency session of the Legislature, and with grace and a bit of self-deprecating humor, he proposed the withholding tax. A faulty heating system made a racket at the press conference where he was announcing his turnaround. The noise, he quipped, was the sound of the cement breaking around his feet. The audience roared. Later, the capital press corps made a gift to Reagan

— a pair of his own brown shoes, obtained from his wife, set in cement. For a long time he kept the memento in his office.

Similarly, he cut his political losses quickly last summer when his effort to recruit Gerald Ford as his vice-presidential running mate fell through late on the third night of the Republican Convention in Detroit. Approving a consensus of his political advisers, he moved quickly to choose George Bush. Then, following his own political instincts against the advice of his convention floor manager, Bill Timmons, and his friend, Senator Paul Laxalt, he broke political tradition and made a midnight appearance at the convention hall, which had excitedly been awaiting word of a Reagan-Ford ticket. Reagan announced that his choice was Bush. His action stunned the hall, but it forestalled an insurrection by disgruntled conservatives and prevented overnight headlines focused on the unhappy ending of his unprecedented negotiations with Ford over the Vice-Presidency.

Surprisingly, perhaps, Reagan has never been a politician's politician with a love of legislative maneuver. He's an orator, a standard-bearer, a performer who thrives on playing to the crowds and a storyteller who enjoys getting off a good joke or a one-liner. But he is not by habit or instinct a member of the fraternity of politicians. In California, he did not seem to enjoy the horse trading, back slapping style of state house politicians nor did he frequent their haunts. Aides had to prod him to show up at political receptions to break the ice. For a long time, he was a loner, much like Jimmy Carter.

"The first year or two of Reagan's administration in California was a disaster," recalled Bill Bagley, a moderate Republican who served one term as Assembly Speaker. "The Reagan crowd ran against the government and against Sacramento and they came in on their white horses and railed against the Legislature. The people around the Governor didn't like us. In their view, we were the hacks he'd run against and we didn't like being treated that way."

But ultimately Reagan began to mix a bit, and, at the start of his second term, he struck a deal with Bob Moretti, the Democratic Speaker of the new Assembly, on the welfare reform program. That proved a model for numerous legislative compromises that served him well. And like Jimmy Carter, Reagan told audiences during the campaign that he felt he could handle Congress because he had successfully handled his state Legislature back home.

Actually, Carter once told a joke on himself for being so naive. He said he'd been advised by friends to treat Congress like the Georgia Legislature. "I tried it," he said, "and they treated me like the Governor of Georgia." In other words, he got nowhere.

There is a considerable difference between Reagan's experience in California and Carter's in Georgia, however. California is a vigorous two-party state with a nearly full-time Legislature, whereas Carter had to deal essentially with a one-party, part-time Legislature. In six of his eight years, Reagan was working with a Legislature controlled by the opposition party, which is what he now faces in one house of Congress. Moreover, as one of the most liberal states in the union, California was a setting where Reagan, even as a conservative, had to accept many social programs on a scale unheard of in Georgia. Nevertheless, he still faces a far more potent and diverse power structure in Congress than he dealt with in his home state.

Republican control of the Senate will help Reagan muster majorities in that chamber. In the House, he enjoys a philosophical majority of conservatives. At least initially, the mainstream Democrats, sensitive to the election returns, may let Reagan largely have his way so that he cannot go to the voters with the complaint that the Democrats are obstructing his programs and defying the popular will.

The early maneuvering of the new Congress may have been foreshadowed by the tactics of the House Budget Committee in the 1980 lame-duck session. By writing some of Reagan's tax cut pledges into the committee's budget resolution but leaving it up to Reagan to make the actual cuts, the Democrats felt they saw an advantage in putting the monkey on Reagan's back to deliver on his campaign promises. Some are skeptical that he can do it. But if this tactic prompts Reagan to cut too deeply into popular social programs or he presses ahead too rapidly with plans to dismantle the Department of Education and the Department of Energy, that may galvanize the Democrats fairly quickly and test how well Reagan copes with determined legislative opposition.

Mindful of his need for support from across the political aisle, Reagan began disarming potential adversaries by talking right after the election about the need for bipartisan foreign policy. He named three Democratic conservatives, Senator Henry M. Jackson of Washington, the recently defeated Senator Richard Stone of Florida, and Jeane Kirkpatrick, a Georgetown University political scientist, to his foreign policy advisory board. On his first political visit to Washington, before Thanksgiving, he made a point of meeting with Democratic Congressional leaders as well as Republicans, a sign that he recalled from his Sacramento days the political benefits of courting the opposition as well as his own partisans.

Paradoxical as it sounds, Reagan may have won too much of a good thing when the Republicans gained control of the Senate. He cannot blame the Democrats for any failures in that body, and it will take considerable dexterity to mold fifty-three Republicans from all points on the ideological spectrum into an effective working majority for his principal objectives.

So long have the Republicans been in the minority that the upstart habits of dissent and opposition may die hard. A few liberals and moderates, like Senator Hatfield of Oregon, sent out early signals that they were unhappy with the Reagan approach on defense and budget-cutting. But initially Republican conservatives may be more of a headache, by going off on tangents and firing up divisive controversies over what, for Reagan, as President, will be side issues.

No sooner had the election returns been tabulated, for example, than conservatives like Strom Thurmond, Jake Garn, and Orrin Hatch were sounding off with the enthusiasm of rookies in spring training about the need to restore capital punishment and school prayers and to abolish guaranteed wage rates at Federal construction sites. Thurmond and Jesse Helms of North Carolina pushed through the Senate a rider on an appropriations bill to bar the Justice Department from entering suits to use busing to improve racial balance in schools. That set off squawks from Republican as well as Democratic liberals that affirmative action programs would be in jeopardy from the new right-wing strength.

The list of potentially emotional side issues is almost endless. And if Reagan gets dragged into such political byways, he may find that he has wasted his early political capital and that his major initiatives are in trouble because he has alienated either his conservative hardcore or the moderates whose support is vital on the big votes.

Much of the blueprint for the Reagan Presidency is borrowed from his California years. Reviving themes from 1966, Reagan has pledged to freeze government hiring and to squeeze 7 to 10 percent in savings from the Federal budget over four years through greater efficiency. As in California, he has moved to set up citizen task forces to scour the Federal system for mismanagement, waste, and fraud, and he immediately appointed his former California Finance Director, Caspar ("Cap the Knife") Weinberger, to use his cutting shears on the 1981 Federal budget.

As a campaigner, Reagan loved to point out that California is the world's seventh largest economy and that, as Governor, he occupied the second biggest executive job in American politics. But there are enormous differences between Sacramento and Washington. In California, Reagan did not have to deal with foreign affairs, manage the defense establishment, or take responsibility for the health of the national economy, his three most consuming tasks as President. In part, at least, his state's prosperity and his tax rebates were a dividend of booming times that owed little to his own policies and that no longer exist to simplify the policy choices he must make as President. Even if the economy has a mild upward blip as he takes office, it is now up to Reagan and his economic advisers to engineer sustained growth in order to do all that he has promised.

The sheer sprawling size and complexity of the Federal estab-lishment and the competing interests of its vast Cabinet depart-ments defy easy control and coordination. As Governor, Reagan could issue line-item vetoes, striking out specific programs from the budget, but he has no such authority in the White House. He must bargain and trade as the budget wriggles through Congress, then accept or reject it, all in huge departmental chunks. At the state level, too, Reagan had more legal power and flexibility in dealing with the civil service than he will at the Federal level. Politically, he now faces entrenched alliances of Federal bureau-crats, Congressional committees, and special interests — what an-other former Governor called "the iron triangle" — ready to blunt his plans to cut programs, dismantle agencies, and turn over some Federal functions to the states.

Whatever the obstacles, Reagan has decided to put the imprint of his own corporate style of leadership on Washington. He is transplanting one central element of his Sacramento experience — his use of a small inner Cabinet as his principal policy-making body. As a political chairman of the board, Reagan liked to meet regularly with his five principal Cabinet officers and his chief of staff, making the thirty-two other state department heads report to him through this inner core. Those small Cabinet meetings were his forum for debating policy options with his closest advisers. As they argued, Reagan would often ply the participants with jelly beans, his favorite candy, or amuse them with one-liners to ease the tension if the arguments got too heavy. Sometimes he would make decisions on the spot, sometimes later. And he delegated to the Cabinet officers the responsibility to carry out his decisions.

Reagan and his aides took one look at the current style of Federal Cabinet meetings — sometimes attended by twenty-five people including department heads, the Budget Director, C.I.A. Director, trade representative, United Nations Ambassador, eco-nomic adviser, White House Chief of Staff, and other aides — and decided they were too unwieldy, too large for the kind of candid give-and-take that Reagan wanted. So they adapted the Sacra-mento model and came up with an Executive Committee of the

Cabinet, seven or eight key figures like the Vice-President, the Attorney General, the Secretaries of State, Treasury, Defense, Agriculture, and Health and Human Services — plus Ed Meese, Reagan's California chief of staff now acting as a Counselor to the President and coordinator of Cabinet business and running the staffs that write up policy options for the Cabinet.

To emphasize the collegial character of the Cabinet and the primary function of its members to advise the President on policy matters across-the-board rather than to act as advocates for the departments they head, the Reagan blueprint called for Cabinet Secretaries to take offices in the Executive Office Building next door to the White House. "Geography is important in Washington," explained one Reagan aide. "The location of their offices is a symbolic move."

Moreover, Meese contended, the Reagan scheme will hopefully reduce the "built-in" competition over policy-making between the Cabinet and a powerful White House staff, a rivalry that has hampered previous administrations. The small inner Cabinet, suggested William French Smith, Reagan's close friend and personal attorney, "provides a diversity of input but is not so large that it's unmanageable." And once the Cabinet officers have had their say, their chance to dissent, he added, they are tacitly committed to loyalty on all presidential decisions.

No less experienced a figure than former President Nixon, who once entertained the idea of a super-Cabinet himself, is skeptical. It is unrealistic, Nixon has said, to expect collective Cabinet responsibility on the British model. "Every new President takes office promising a strong Cabinet of independent members and some new Presidents take office really believing this promise," Nixon wrote in a *Time* magazine essay this fall. "But each soon learns that there have to be limits on the individual Cabinet members' independence, and that the Cabinet as a collective body is not suited to decision-making. . . . Each department is a separate fiefdom; if there is to be coherence and direction to the administration's policies, the President has to impose that direction from the top, cutting across the often conflicting interests of the various departments. The President must, of course, consult his Cabinet members, just as he consults the leaders of Congress. But on the larger questions only he can decide; only he can lead."

In the past, the Reagan approach has put a heavy premium on the calibre and experience of his principal advisers. Some who have worked with him, like John Sears, contend that Reagan's dependence on his Cabinet and staff makes him, in essence, the captive of his inner circle. They see him as a leader who ratifies the consensus of his closest advisers on many decisions rather than originating his decisions in lonely isolation, as Nixon did, or by forcing the clash of competing ideas from individual advisers, operating on their own, as Franklin D. Roosevelt did.

"Reagan sits at any gathering of close advisers as an interested participant rather than as the leader who orders the discussion," Sears commented. "He's not a stupid man. He appreciates the nuances of what is proposed to him. It's just that he's not the originator of ideas. He's a more malleable and moderate person than he's generally thought to be. He's not a conceptualizer. He's a borrower and an endorser. It's fair to say that on some occasions he is presented with options and selects one, but it is also true that in other instances he simply looks to someone to tell him what to do."

Sears' theory is that Reagan learned to accept the advice of handlers during his long years as an actor in Hollywood when producers and directors gave him a script and told him what role to play. Sears cites his own experience in persuading Reagan to accept Schweiker as his 1976 running mate or to go along with the cautious, blenderized, aloof style of campaigning at the start of 1980, though when that failed, Reagan angrily dismissed Sears at the urging of conservatives. Later, a subsequent group of advisers pushed Reagan first to keep, then to get rid of Republican National Chairman Bill Brock, and finally to retain him when that stirred up opposition among Republican regulars. It was his campaign staff, too, that persuaded him, despite his initial reluctance, to try first Ford and then Bush as his running mate. In each case, Reagan was moved by the consensus of his staff or close friends.

"It is the endorsing process that accounts for the difference between Reagan, the campaigner, and Reagan's more moderate record as Governor of California," Sears wrote in *The Washington Post* last summer. "The white-carded stump speeches are Reagan, the performer, playing to a known audience and sending the crowd away with its money's worth. As Governor, there was no crowd, merely decisions to be made, only a few of which were very exciting. Reagan sat with his California Cabinet more as an equal than as its leader. Once consensus was derived or conflict resolved, he emerged as spokesman."

Others who worked with Reagan during that period strongly dispute Sears' portrait. "If it's a routine decision, it's probably true that Reagan goes along with a consensus," comments William French Smith, a California attorney who served with Reagan on the University of California Board of Regents for several years. "But believe me, he's anything but a rubber stamp. The whole Board of Regents could go one way and he'd go the other way if he felt strongly. He'd overrule the whole group without batting an eye. What's more, he'll make a decision promptly and decisively, and never look back."

Others say that Reagan has often received divided counsel but this has not paralyzed him from making decisions. As Governor he was urged by some Cabinet aides to order construction of Dos Rios Dam in northern California as a flood and water control measure in the Round Valley region. Cabinet opponents argued against the project on grounds it would destroy a very picturesque area and violate a treaty with Indians living there. In the end, Reagan decided against the dam. "He didn't want to go against the Indian treaties," recalls Ed Meese.

In the 1980 campaign, Reagan insisted, against the advice of his political aides, on backing a constitutional amendment banning abortions. Later, some advisers urged him to back away from his plan for a three-year, across-the-board 10 percent annual income tax cut, but Reagan stuck with it. Finally, he received conflicting advice on whether he should debate Carter this fall and came down quickly on the side of the pro-debate majority on his staff.

Like Eisenhower, Reagan likes to get his information for decisions orally or in very short memos. "He likes to sit down and listen to the arguments," says Ed Meese. "He feels that in the adversary situation, in the contest of ideas, you get the best possible ideas and the widest scope and variety of action. If you're just reading, it's only two-dimensional. But orally, it allows him to question the participants. One idea sparks another. Having a meeting creates a focal point for decision-making. You get the key policy advisers and after they've had an input, it builds teamwork."

In California, he liked one-page cover memos on the staff papers that came to him. His executive assistant, William Clark, devised a system of "mini memos" four paragraphs long, with the first paragraph stating the issue, the second setting out the facts, the third providing analysis, and the fourth a conclusion or a recommendation. The memos were no more than 300 to 400 words long. At the bottom, if he agreed, Reagan could initial "O.K. R.R." On a critical policy question, Reagan would get a stream of mini memos, 100 or more, keeping him abreast of a changing situation. Sometimes they were accompanied by long staff studies.

"This guy does his homework and comes back with questions that indicate he's thought about what his staff gives him to read," said Richard Whalen, a Reagan consultant and speechwriter. "He identifies his concerns as he reads. But he likes to get his information face-to-face. He likes to look at people and ask them questions."

There is a contrary, though minority, view of Reagan, that he is sometimes not sufficiently demanding of those who brief him. "To a certain extent, he wants confirmation and amplification of his own views," said one former aide. "His operational inclination is not to say, 'I want to know the other side. I want to know the subtleties.' He's read a lot over the years and he thinks he knows."

This former aide suggested that the fault lay with subordinates reluctant to give Reagan bad news. "Most people around big politicians are intimidated by power and the people around Reagan are no exception," this man observed. "Reagan will take contrary advice if you give it to him well. You have to be sharp and persuasive. He'll lose his temper. Or his eyes will glaze over if people give him a lot of generalities. He gets bored with a lot of baloney. You've got to push him. You've got to be firm. You have to tell him, 'You've been wrong, Governor,' or 'You ought to take this more into account,' or 'Governor, you ought to put it this way.' He doesn't like it, but he'll take it. I'm not sure that some of the people around him are always up to that."

Reagan has several circles of advisers. The most forthright and most trusted are his California Kitchen Cabinet. These are his peers, the old political and social friends with whom he relaxes and to whom he turns in a crunch: Justin Dart, the industrialist; Holmes Tuttle, owner of several Los Angeles automobile dealerships; William French Smith, his personal attorney; and others. They coaxed him into politics, helped pick his Sacramento Cabinet in 1966, and did the same job again this time. They also nudged him into picking George Bush as Vice-President, as a smart political move that would sit well with the business community.

These are Reagan's most reliable and most oft-used sounding board and, in large measure, they tend to reinforce his own view of the world, especially his faith in free enterprise, his distaste for big government, and his wary suspicion of world Communism. In terms of personality, at one end is Dart, a bulky, gruff, blunt-spoken but likable self-made sunbelt enterpreneur still vigorous at seventy-two; and at the other end is Smith, a trim, precise, composed, thoughtful, even bookish and worldly attorney with proper Bostonian roots.

Reagan's campaign advisers are about a generation younger than the Kitchen Cabinet. They are mostly men in their mid-forties and early fifties with personal businesses that they left for the campaign but did not want to give up for the White House. Most are political technicians and tacticians rather than policy advisers. Typical of that group is Michael K. Deaver, Reagan's campaign tour director. Deaver is a smooth, self-controlled professional and Reagan loyalist with a private public relations firm in Los Angeles and with close enough ties to Reagan, dating back to his staff as Governor, to serve the new President as a personal aide.

By far the most important of this group and the one to whom Reagan turns most instinctively is Edwin Meese, III, his former California chief of staff. Meese is an attorney with a bent for management and an interest in police work, now on leave from his post as Director of the Center for Criminal Justice Policy and Management at the University of San Diego law school. He is so management-oriented and thinks so readily in terms of administrative structures that he frequently refers to the President's 300 most important political appointees as the "300 top managerial jobs" in government.

Cordial, methodical, and unflappable, Meese, now forty-nine, has sometimes been criticized by colleagues as indecisive, overly neutral, and disinclined to give Reagan contrary advice. But he has a good public presence, a friendly manner, a quick mind, and organizational skill. Reagan is comfortable with Meese as his most handy collator and coordinator of options. His role as the President's counselor working with the Cabinet on issues makes him, as he once said, "the pivot point" of the new administration. In no other aide does Reagan repose greater confidence, and that is why he has chosen to put Meese at his elbow.

A top Carter White House official came away from his first encounter with Meese and other leaders of the Reagan transition team impressed with their calibre, their knowledgeability, and their calm self-assurance.

"They're good," said this lifelong Democrat. "They're experienced. They know what they're doing and they know what they want. They're better informed than we were four years ago. They're older than we were, less awed and excited about taking over the government. A lot of them are Washington veterans. But out of twenty-four people, there were only two women. No blacks and no other minorities. They're more relaxed about their work than we were. I have a feeling this White House is going to have a hell of a lot more fun than we did. They're going to have wine for lunch. There's going to be an atmospheric change for the better inside the government. Now, whether that will work to the good of the country remains to be seen."

Among politicians, Reagan's closest friend and confidant is Senator Paul Laxalt of Nevada. Had Reagan had an entirely free hand, without having to worry about geographical balance or ideological diversity or name recognition among voters, he would have picked Laxalt as his Vice-President. That would have delighted his conservative partisans.

Politics dictated Bush, who in his tireless, upbeat eagerness had proven Reagan's most effective challenger. Bush's experience as U.N. Ambassador, chief American diplomat in Peking, and Director of Central Intelligence compensated for Reagan's lack of experience in foreign affairs. With the election over, Reagan has talked of using Bush as more than a ceremonial stand-in and the presiding officer of the Senate. Not to draw Bush into policy formulation and into the Cabinet, Reagan said rather drily at his first post-election press conference, would be to "waste a valuable asset." Each has spoken of their growing friendship and their regular contacts by phone during the campaign, and obviously they get on well enough. But Bush's role has not been defined and they are very different men, Bush with his Connecticut Yankee roots to the Eastern Establishment and Reagan with his roots in the Midwest and his life shaped by Hollywood. It will take time for them to forge a full working partnership.

Reagan's friendship with Laxalt, on the other hand, springs from an instinctive personal camaraderie and conservative ideological kinship. They met in 1966 as governors of neighboring states and immediately became friends. Laxalt, the son of a Basque sheepherder who immigrated to this country, is an open, gregarious, striking, silver-haired Westerner given to wearing well-polished boots with his tailored suits. He led the opposition to the Panama Canal Treaties, motivated by concern about national defense, but he avoided the emotionalism of other treaty foes. In the Senate, he is known for his mild manner and sensitivity to others' feelings.

Twice, Laxalt has talked Reagan into making his runs for the Presidency and has become chairman of the Reagan campaigns. In the Senate, he is the uncrowned leader of the conservatives, a man who could have made a bid this year for the Senate leadership but understood at once that it would be divisive and chose not to. Membership in the Reagan Cabinet could have easily been his, though he felt he could help Reagan more in the Senate by managing and channeling feisty conservatives. So close is Laxalt to the new President that Howard Baker shrewdly observed, "Paul is the one person whose position is so secure that he doesn't need a title in the new administration."

As Reagan turned to the business of picking his Cabinet, he was looking for a mix of leaders with Washington experience, fresh political faces, and expert managers drawn from the world of business. He wanted what Meese called "independent players who will voice dissenting views" but within the framework of his conservative philosophy. "Obviously," said Meese, "he doesn't want to debate the basics in Cabinet meetings. What he likes are people who will speak their minds — but team players, not dissenters who leak to the press various options that weren't taken." Quite deliberately Reagan staffed his various advisory panels with Cabinet candidates.

In the most controversial field, economic policy, Reagan has borrowed heavily from the populist "supply side" economics of Representative Jack Kemp of Buffalo and California economist Arthur Laffer, but the lead in his economic advisory group has been taken by more traditional conservatives like former Treasury Secretary George Shultz; Alan Greenspan, former Chairman of the Council of Economic Advisers; and William Simon, the former Treasury Secretary who is a favorite of Reagan's Kitchen Cabinet. When he sought advice on spending cuts, he chose Caspar Weinberger, a former Federal Budget Director with experience and qualifications to take on one of several Cabinet-level jobs.

Reagan put his foreign policy advisory board under William J. Casey, a sixty-seven-year old New York tax lawyer who ran his campaign, has a long background in intelligence, and served as Undersecretary of State for Economic Affairs. As time wore on, Reagan leaned heavily on former Nixon and Ford administration officials like former NATO Commander and White House Staff Chief, Al Haig, former Secretary of State Henry Kissinger, former Treasury Secretary and Texas Governor John B. Connally, former Defense Secretary Donald Rumsfeld, and Senator John Tower of Texas, the ranking Republican on the Armed Services Committee. He also made a point of drawing a Democrat, Senator Henry M. Jackson of Washington, into his senior council.

The Reagan team had a problem finding many blacks and women for top spots. But among the blacks were Thomas Sowell, a conservative economist from the University of California at Los Angeles, and Walter E. Williams, another economist from Temple University. One or the other has taken the kind of positions Reagan advocates by opposing the minimum wage, busing, and affirmative action programs. Among the women singled out by the Reagan high command were Anne Armstrong, former U.S. Ambassador to Britain; Jeane Kirkpatrick, a political scientist and a conservative Democrat; and Elizabeth Dole, a former member of the Federal Trade Commission.

Reagan's best known woman adviser, however, is his wife, Nancy, who is such a constant companion that one friend jokingly remarked, "They are joined at the hip." Their very closeness has fueled speculation and controversy about her political influence on Reagan. She has denied having influenced his conversion from Democratic liberalism to Republican conservativism in the postwar period, having affected his views on policy matters, or having engineered any of the various changes in his staff over the years. "My husband makes his decisions," she told a *New York Times* interviewer. "I might suggest an idea to him, but my husband makes his decisions."

Other politicians, especially those who have worked closely around Reagan, believe that she reinforces his opposition to the Equal Rights Amendment and to abortion, but otherwise has limited influence on issues. Where they sense her weight is on his choice of staff or his broader political strategy. Many believe she was more eager for him to run for the Presidency in 1976 than Reagan himself. "She's very much involved in most of the major decisions of the campaign, as a key adviser to the Governor," commented Charles Black, national political director for Reagan before his staff purge in February 1980. "He's his own man, but she's probably the single most important influence on him. And she's very ambitious for him, as well as totally dedicated."

John Sears described her principal role as one of a sounding board, not so much telling Reagan what to do or not to do but responding to his various alternatives. "It's more helping him talk something through because she knows him better than anyone else," Sears said. Others have described her as a keener, quicker judge of people than Reagan, and thus an important influence on his choice of top advisers or his running mate. They attribute to her a major role in his decision, for example, to let go his Press Secretary, Lyn Nofziger, and even to fire Sears, Black, and Jim Lake during the primary campaign after his Iowa loss. And most of his entourage regard it as very important for any top Reagan adviser to be on the good side of Nancy. "She's quicker and surer in her judgments of people than Reagan is," said one aide, "and that's something on which he listens to her and is affected by her judgments. If she likes someone, it can help. If she doesn't think much of someone, it can hurt."

"Has she influenced me?" Reagan himself responded when asked the question. "Yes, because I've never been happier in my life than I have been with her. She is very much what you see. There is a gentleness to her, a fierce feeling of family loyalty. I miss her very much when we're not together. We're very happy. I

177

imagine if I sold shoes, as my father did, she would have wanted to help me sell shoes. She's a very intelligent person. I don't know of anything we don't talk about."

Ronald Wilson Reagan has promised the American people no less than "an era of national renewal" and the election of 1980 has provided him a more favorable setting for a bold experiment in conservatism than either he or his partisans had dreamed of. The Republicans, surprised by their own success, sense a unique opportunity that must not be squandered by shooting off on controversial tangents. The Democrats, chastened by their losses, are prepared to give the new President a chance provided he does not go too far to undo the social programs of the past two decades. And Reagan, himself, in his first moves, has been sensitive enough to reach beyond his California circle for top-level talent and to signal immediate interest in marshalling as broad a bipartisan coalition as possible to carry forward his objectives.

On his first post-election visit to Washington, Reagan charmed the political establishment, which was flattered by his attention. "I like him," said House Speaker Thomas P. O'Neill, Jr. "He left an amiable feeling." With a bit of symbolism widely appreciated as a contrast with Jimmy Carter, who ran for President as an outsider and remained an outsider to much of the city, Reagan quickly offered the hand of friendship to the city's civic leaders and local Democrats by hosting prominent business, cultural and political figures at a dinner in the exclusive, Victorian F. Street Club.

"Now you're in the big leagues," O'Neill told Reagan jokingly. "He was a little surprised when I said that," the speaker observed afterward. "That won't be the first time he'll be surprised."

Reagan has awakened extravagant expectations and if he is to succeed he will need not only a well united party behind him but time — time to try to curb inflation, rekindle the productive thrust of the economy, restore the nation's sense of military security, relieve its fearful and inflationary dependence on foreign oil, and revamp the role of the Federal Government in American life. The problems that confront him will take years to solve and the solutions he proposes will take years to work, more time perhaps than an impatient and undisciplined public will allow, more time than a turbulent world may permit.

The time imperative presses Reagan to produce an immediate sense of forward motion, to produce the feeling that he is taking charge of the situation, that something is being done to cope with the drift and uncertainty that caused such an explosive burst of frustration from the voters against Jimmy Carter and the Democrats on November 4.

With the sense of that urgency, the new administration is following a timetable that calls for a freeze on Federal hiring and a dramatic package of cuts in the 1981 budget within ten days of inauguration, quickly followed by messages to Congress promoting Reagan's 10 percent income tax cut and accelerated business depreciation schedules to stimulate the private sector, and another message asking renewal of presidential authority to reorganize executive departments, laying the groundwork to carry out Reagan's campaign pledge to abolish the Department of Education and possibly the Department of Energy as well. By executive order, Reagan and his Cabinet will quickly begin snipping away at the web of regulations that strangles economic growth, as Reagan sees it. Decontrol of oil pricing may be speeded up.

Symbolically, Reagan's advisers believe, the most important action is the drive to hold down Federal spending to cutbacks in Federal travel, outside consulting contracts, and the purchase of equipment, as well as stretching out expenditures for highways, airports, mass transit, and sewage plants, not to mention potential savings through trimming eligibility rules and overlapping payments in the food stamp program, school lunch program, housing assistance and Medicaid. "We'll never bring down long-term interest rates unless we show the financial markets we mean business," said Representative Jack Kemp, an ardent advocate of incentive economics.

Reagan's dilemma is that if the cutbacks are too sharp, he will arouse the powerful combined opposition of many interest groups and then embroil his proposals in legislative dogfights and delays, but if they are not sharp enough, that will undermine his basic economic strategy. "If Reagan can improve the efficiency of the Federal government without hurting benefits, there isn't a Democrat who doesn't want to do that," said Representative Thomas Foley of Washington, in a characteristic mainstream Democratic reaction. "But if the administration moves in radical ways to undo programs enacted over the last two generations, there will be opposition."

Even before taking office, the Reagan strategists recognize that tampering with the Social Security program would be political suicide. Moreover, Ed Meese among others recalled that Jimmy Carter, in his ambitions for an energetic Presidency, had contributed to his own undoing by overloading Congress in his first months in office. "It's a big mistake to try to do too much immediately after taking office," Meese observed. "We want to pace ourselves and keep a firm sense of priorities." But the high priority attached by Reagan to a big rise in defense spending, if accompanied by drastic domestic cuts, may touch off a troubling groundswell in Congress that will nag him for months to come.

Reagan himself, seeking greater public patience, remarked that "those things we can do administratively, we'll start doing immediately, but I don't think we've ever promised the effect will be immediate."

One difficulty is that Reagan is bound to be caught in a cross fire between hesitant Democrats like Foley and ardent Reaganites of the New Right who want strong action and are irked by any hint that Reagan is letting what he once called "pale pastels" creep into "the bold banner" of conservatism that he held aloft for years. "I don't see the hardcore Reaganites around Reagan," said John Lofton, editor of *Conservative Digest*. "Sometimes I wonder how much of a Reaganite Reagan is, and unfortunately those times are becoming more frequent."

In his battle for time, the new President has one great asset over Jimmy Carter: his capacity to use what Teddy Roosevelt called "the bully pulpit" to communicate his vision to the people and to replenish his political power by rallying popular support.

Some have called Reagan the most effective media politician of the McLuhan era. So far, his political mastery has not been of the people in the political structure, but of the camera, the scene, the techniques of mass communication. As Hollywood discovered, he is a natural-born star. In an era of media-dominated politics, in which all office seekers and officeholders are actors to some degree, Reagan has the advantage of the professional. As Jimmy Carter discovered in what for him was their devastating debate in Cleveland, Reagan is at home on stage and has been for years.

But this is not an unalloyed asset for Reagan; he cannot afford to misuse it. As the verbal gaffes of his fall campaign indicated, he may trip up and in the White House, stumbles can be very, very costly. For the Presidency invites demanding scrutiny to every word and Reagan can no longer afford to do freely, without discipline, what he has done best all these years — play to sympathetic conservative audiences, occasionally giving them what some of his campaign aides have graphically termed "a piece of red meat" in the form of hot political rhetoric. Careless words can upset diplomacy abroad or undercut credibility at home, especially for a leader who banks heavily on his speeches to generate the momentum behind his programs.

"In the first year or so, Reagan will probably get along all right with the kind of general approach he used in the campaign," commented a Carter White House official. "But what is he going to do after his first year, when the people see the problems are now his and not Carter's anymore? How is he going to use one-liners at that point to explain the complexities of the situation?"

The sense of momentum is with the Republicans now as they take office, but Reagan's own aides are mindful that it will take special effort to control the potential divisions in the Republican ranks on Capitol Hill in the months ahead. And further afield, events beyond Reagan's control may conspire to distract him from his central purpose. The rioting among blacks in Miami, Florida, last spring was an indicator that frustration among minorities, especially if they feel neglected by local and national leadership, can erupt at any time. Food prices can suddenly shoot up because of shortages or OPEC may hike oil prices and play havoc with Reagan's anti-inflation program. For philosophic reasons, Reagan has refused to use direct measures to stem the steady upward march of domestic wages and prices.

Like other Presidents, Reagan is following his first impulse to turn inward, to nurse domestic ills first and let the world wait. When he was asked by *Time* magazine right after his election about the prospects for arms negotiations with the Soviets, his response was: "The first job is to let them see the course we were going to follow domestically, getting hold of our economy, straightening out our energy problems. And the fact that we have the will and determination to add to our defensive stature."

The Kremlin may or may not choose to wait and be satisfied with slow-moving preparations for arms talk and a rather cool relationship with Washington. And in waiting, the Soviets may become more responsive to the Reagan approach or else more aggressive in the third world, more inclined to prey upon divisions in the Atlantic Alliance, and less inhibited about intervening in Poland if that situation gets out of hand again. But even if Moscow is patient, Reagan will be a fortunate President indeed if he is not embroiled in some confrontation with Iran, some provocative widening of the Iran-Iraq war, some awkward Arab-Israeli flare-up, some worrisome upheaval in the Caribbean, or an economic test of strength with OPEC over new oil price increases. As Jimmy Carter found out, the world will not cooperate with a President's calendar.

In short, it will take good fortune, consummate political skill, a clear set of priorities focused primarily on the economy, and an ability to hold together the political coalition in Congress and the popular support among the electorate, if Reagan is to make good on the promise of his stunning electoral victory. Above all else, his formula for managing the economy must produce tangible results within a couple of years.

"I think we have the opportunity to do what Konrad Adenauer did in Germany, to become the party of peace and prosperity that remains in power for two generations," said Jack Kemp, one of Reagan's most enthusiastic backers. "But up to now it's been just campaign rhetoric. We'll be a majority party when we implement the policies that will bring about the prosperity and full employment without inflation we have promised. If we fail, this will not turn out to be a significant election."

Chronology

February 6, 1911	Born in Tampico, Illinois, son of Jack and Nelle Reagan
1920	Reagan family moves to Dixon, Illinois, 90 miles west of Chicago, where he will attend North High School
1932	Graduates from Eureka College with a major in economics Hired as a $10-a-game, play-by-play announcer at radio station WOC in Davenport, Iowa
1933	Takes a job as $75-a-week sportscaster at WHO in Des Moines, Iowa
1937	Signed by Warner Brothers, he makes his film debut playing a radio announcer in *Love Is on the Air*
1940	Marries Jane Wyman Portrays George Gipp in *Knute Rockne, All-American*
1941	Daughter Maureen is born
1942	Appears in *King's Row*, the highlight of his film career
1942-1945	Serves in the U.S. Army Air Corps, attaining the rank of captain
1945	Adopts a son, Michael

1947	Elected to the first of six terms as president of the Screen Actors Guild
	Testifies as a friendly witness in the House Un-American Activities Committee probe of the movie industry
1948	Marriage to Jane Wyman ends in divorce
1950	Campaigns for Helen Gahagan Douglas in her unsuccessful Senate race against Richard Nixon
1952	Marries Nancy Davis on March 4
	Daughter Patricia is born
1954-1962	Host of *General Electric Theater* on television and spokesman for General Electric's personnel-relations program
1958	Son Ronald is born
1962	Switches political affiliation to the Republican Party
1964	Final film appearance, in *The Killers*
	Gains national attention in October through his televised "A Time to Choose" address on behalf of Republican presidential candidate Barry Goldwater
1965	Autobiography, *Where's the Rest of Me?* (with Richard G. Hubler), published
1966	Elected governor of California
1968	Makes a last-minute run for the Republican presidential nomination and is defeated by Richard Nixon.
1970	Reelected to second term as governor of California
1976	Narrowly defeated for Republican presidential nomination by incumbent President Gerald R. Ford
1980	Wins the Republican nomination for the Presidency, with George Bush as his running mate
November 4, 1980	Elected 40th President of the United States